AQA Fun
Maths

Tony Fisher
June Haighton
Kathryn Scott
Veronica Thomas
Margaret Thornton

Series Editor:
Paul Metcalf

Nelson Thornes

Published in 2008 by:
Nelson Thornes Ltd
Delta Place
27 Bath Road
CHELTENHAM
GL53 7TH
United Kingdom

08 09 10 11 12 / 10 9 8 7 6 5 4 3 2 1

A catalogue record for this book is available from the British Library

ISBN 978 0 7487 9980 0

Cover photograph © Nelson Thornes Ltd

Illustrations by Viners Wood Associates

Page make-up by Viners Wood Associates

Printed and bound in Scotland by Scotprint

Acknowledgements

Photos
p4: University students (5004550) © iStock; pp 6–7: Teenagers in school uniform (AJPHYG) © Design Pics Inc/Alamy; p10: Blue sky and clouds image reproduced with permission; p11: Weathervane (2135445) © iStock; p12: Train image reproduced with permission; p16: Fuel economy label reprinted with the kind permission of the VCA www.vca.gov.uk; Information for the vehicle tax table collated and produced with the permission of the DVLA; p17: Traffic queue (4799612) © iStock; p19: Cartoon by Geoff McNeill reproduced with permission www.CartoonStock.com; p22: Female dentist with young patient (4700087) © iStock; p24: Vegetables (5203941) © iStock; p25: Quiche (3193445) © iStock; p28: Exercise machine (4328590) © iStock; p30: Scooters © Radu Razvan/Photolia; p34: Chicken nibblers © Ingram Food Menu (NT); p35: Chicken wings (5188662) © iStock; p36: Carpets © Kevin Penhallow/Photolia; p40: Games console image © Kirsty Pargeter/Photolia; p42: Hydrangea image reproduced with permission; p43: Trellis image reproduced with permission; p46: Skateboarder (3421349) © iStock; p47: Young boy climbing on a wall (AEWCXK – L) © Stefan Sollfers/Alamy; p48: Lionhead goldfish (2452213) © iStock; Common goldfish (3825382) © iStock; p52: Chimney stack and television aerial (4069830) © iStock; p54: Petrol station and shop (2993597) © iStock; p57: Man filling car with fuel (3865368) © iStock; p58: Tyre marks (265146) © iStock; p59: Speed camera (4897068) © iStock; pp60 and 62: Bus driver (5617246) © iStock; p64: Aeroplane (4715258) © iStock; pp66–67: Countryside (3880338) © iStock; p69: Compass (5057518) © iStock; p70: Internet bid (4493185) © iStock; p72: Alphabet puzzle (5210153) © iStock; pp76–77: University students (5004550) © iStock.

Text
Page 60: Bus and ferry timetables reproduced with permission of Nexus.

Contents

Features of the Student Book

This Student Book has been **written and reviewed by AQA examiners** to support, enhance and extend the learning of functional mathematics. This book covers all areas of the standalone AQA functional mathematics assessment. The functionality paper is supported by two types of task within the book: long tasks containing pre-release data, and shorter tasks (with no pre-release data). The competency paper is supported by questions covering all of the functional standards.

Data Sheets

Long task: based around a pre-release data sheet

Pre-release data sheet
The data sheet used in the task reflects the style and level of material that students will be tested on in the functional mathematics assessment.

Data sheet practice questions
The practice questions act as a warm-up or starter, allowing you to engage with the data sheet and gain confidence with the mathematical skills being tested. Some level 1 material may be included here.

Data sheet questions
Data sheet questions prepare you for the real assessment. Most questions in this section are aimed at level 2.

Extension questions
This set of questions is provided to give you an additional challenge.

Short task: independent of a pre-release data sheet

Main questions
Data sheet questions prepare students for the real assessment. Most questions in this section are aimed at level 2.

Extension questions
This set of questions is provided to give you an additional challenge.

Competency Questions

Provided at the end of the book, competency questions reflect the third part of the functional mathematics assessment. These are short questions with little or no context provided. The questions have been set to test all aspects of the functional mathematics standards for level 2, and use of a calculator for this section is not allowed, since the competency assessment as part of functional mathematics is a non-calculator assessment.

Collecting for charity

Tom and Anna are planning a collection in their school for a local charity.

- They plan to collect from students either in Year 10 or in Year 11.
- Their teachers give them permission to collect the money either on Monday morning (during a Citizenship lesson) or Wednesday afternoon (during an RE lesson).
- They need to decide on the year group and the best day to make the collection.
- To help them do this they collect attendance data for the previous 25 weeks of the school year. Some of this data is not available.

Attendance data for Years 10 and 11

Week	Monday morning		Wednesday afternoon	
	Year 10	Year 11	Year 10	Year 11
1	188	189	192	190
2	184	187	188	192
3	189	193	188	196
4	192	201	190	202
5	188	203	188	202
6	182	203	182	203
7	176	195	186	202
8	178	193	179	198
9	169	201	176	199
10	173	203	177	204
11	188	199	188	200
12	190	199	190	198
13	186	204	188	204
14	181	196	187	196
15	192	202	188	200
16	186	200	184	194
17	188	198	189	189
18	183	197		197
19	176		188	190
20	176	192	182	202
21	182	188	176	194
22	191	199	178	201
23	187		172	199
24	180	203		200
25	172	196	188	201

Pre-release data sheet

Data Sheet Practice

You will need to use the data sheet for **Collecting for charity** to answer these questions.

1. What sort of data is this?

2. How could the Handling Data Cycle be used to decide on the day and year group?

3. The data has been collected to investigate a hypothesis. Give an example of a possible hypothesis.

4. Give examples of how the data might be represented.

5. What measures of average might you use? How do you work them out?

6. What measures of spread might you use? How do you work them out?

7. What other information might be required to help make a decision?

Data Sheet Questions

You will need to use the data sheet for **Collecting for charity** to answer these questions.

1. Which year group has the greater attendance on Monday morning between weeks 1 and 5 inclusive? You **must** show your working.   *(2 marks)*

2. Tom and Anna decide to investigate this hypothesis:

   Attendance is greater on Wednesday afternoon than on Monday morning.

   Write down another hypothesis that Tom and Anna could investigate.   *(1 mark)*

3 Tom and Anna draw these ordered stem-and-leaf diagrams showing the attendances for Year 10 on Monday morning and Wednesday afternoon.

Key: | 17 | 2 represents an attendance of 172

Monday morning

16	9
17	2 3 6 6 6 8
18	0 1 2 2 3 4 6 6 7 8 8 8 8 9
19	0 1 2 2

Wednesday afternoon

16	
17	2 6 6 7 8 9
18	2 2 4 6 7 8 8 8 8 8 8 8 8 9
19	0 0 2

Use the stem-and-leaf diagrams to compare the average attendance and the spread of attendances of Year 10 on Monday morning and Wednesday afternoon. *(2 marks)*

4 **a** Draw ordered stem-and-leaf diagrams to show the attendances for Year 11 on Monday morning and Wednesday afternoon. *(4 marks)*

b Compare the average attendance and the spread of attendances of Year 11 on Monday morning and Wednesday afternoon. *(2 marks)*

5 Tom and Anna ask a random sample of 20 students from each year group how much they are likely to donate to the charity. The table shows the results.

Amount (p, pence)	Year 10	Year 11
$0 \le p < 20$	1	2
$20 \le p < 40$	3	4
$40 \le p < 60$	10	12
$60 \le p < 80$	3	1
$80 \le p < 100$	3	1

Tom and Anna use the table to calculate an estimate of the mean amount that the students in Year 10 and the students in Year 11 are likely to donate.

Their estimate for Year 10 is 54 pence per student.

a Calculate their estimate for Year 11. *(4 marks)*

b Show that your estimate is sensible. *(1 mark)*

6 Use all the evidence to decide whether Tom and Anna should collect from Year 10 or from Year 11 on Monday morning or Wednesday afternoon.
Give a reason for your decision. *(2 marks)*

Extension Questions

Week	% attendance	
	Year 10	Year 11
1	95.9	88.3
2	93.9	87.4
3	96.4	90.2
4	98.0	93.9
5	95.9	94.9
6	92.9	94.9
7	89.8	91.1
8	90.8	90.2
9	86.2	93.9
10	88.3	94.9
11	95.9	93.0
12	96.9	93.0
13	94.9	95.3
14	92.3	91.6
15	98.0	94.4
16	94.9	93.5
17	95.9	92.5
18	93.4	92.1
19	89.8	88.3
20	89.8	89.7
21	92.9	87.9
22	97.4	93.0
23	95.4	94.9
24	91.8	94.9
25	87.8	91.6

The table shows percentage attendances for Years 10 and 11.

1 For each set of attendance data:

(a) Complete a frequency table using class intervals of width 2.
For example, 88 ≤ % attendance < 90
Use your frequency table to draw a frequency polygon.

(b) Calculate an estimate of the mean attendance.

(c) Complete a cumulative frequency table and graph.

(d) Estimate the median and interquartile range.

(e) Draw a box plot using the same horizontal scale.

2 (a) Use your answers to question 1 to compare the attendances of Years 10 and 11.

(b) Comment on the validity of this hypothesis:

Attendance in Year 11 is better than in Year 10.

Weather wise

Weather record for one week in April

Day	Time	Temp	UV index	Rain	Cloud	Wind direction	Wind speed
Monday	Morning	14°C	4	0.1 mm	67%	SW	10 mph
	Afternoon	17°C	2	0.8 mm	100%	SW	13 mph
	Evening	11°C	0	0.7 mm	97%	SW	11 mph
Tuesday	Morning	9°C	0	3.9 mm	100%	SSW	10 mph
	Afternoon	12°C	2	6.1 mm	100%	SSW	11 mph
	Evening	10°C	0	0.1 mm	100%	SSW	11 mph
Wednesday	Morning	8°C	0	4.5 mm	100%	SW	11 mph
	Afternoon	16°C	8	3.4 mm	66%	SW	15 mph
	Evening	7°C	0	0 mm	67%	SSW	11 mph
Thursday	Morning	8°C	2	0 mm	100%	S	9 mph
	Afternoon	17°C	8	0 mm	30%	SSW	10 mph
	Evening	9°C	0	0 mm	99%	SSW	11 mph
Friday	Morning	11°C	1	0.3 mm	100%	SSW	12 mph
	Afternoon	18°C	7	0.1 mm	39%	SW	15 mph
	Evening	9°C	0	0 mm	7%	SW	12 mph
Saturday	Morning	13°C	4	0 mm	47%	SW	11 mph
	Afternoon	19°C	7	0 mm	50%	W	11 mph
	Evening	11°C	0	0 mm	59%	SW	9 mph
Sunday	Morning	16°C	4	0 mm	5%	W	6 mph
	Afternoon	21°C	7	2.9 mm	44%	NW	6 mph
	Evening	13°C	0	4 mm	48%	SW	7 mph

1. The UV index shows the risk of skin damage from the sun's rays. At what time of day is the risk highest? Explain your answer. *(2 marks)*

2. On which day of the week does the temperature drop most between the afternoon and the evening? *(2 marks)*

3. On which day of the week was there the most rainfall? You **must** show your working. *(3 marks)*

4 Meera says that the temperature goes up when the cloud
   cover increases.

   a Give an example of a piece of data that supports
      Meera's theory.   *(1 mark)*

   b Give an example of a piece of data that does not support
      Meera's theory.   *(1 mark)*

5 During the week Josh went for a cycle ride.
   • The wind speed was 11 mph.
   • The UV index was 0.
   • The cloud cover was 100%.
   • There was a lot of rain.
   In which direction was the wind blowing?   *(2 marks)*

Extension Questions

1 a Calculate the mean wind speed over the week.

   b Find the median wind speed over the week.

   c Find the modal wind speed over the week.

   d Draw a vertical bar chart to show the wind speed data and relate what it shows
      to your answers to parts (a), (b) and (c).

2 a Draw a time series graph to represent the temperatures.

   b Calculate the three-point moving averages of the temperatures.

   c Plot the moving averages on the same graph.
      Explain why they show the trend more clearly.

Village bus and train services

A new train station and a new bus service are planned for a village.

A survey was carried out to ask local residents for their opinions about the plans.

The population of the village is 12 000.

All households in the village were sent a survey form.

Replies were received from 800 people.

Replies to some of the questions are summarised in these diagrams.

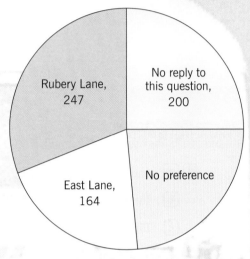

Which location for the new station?

Rubery Lane, 247

No reply to this question, 200

East Lane, 164

No preference

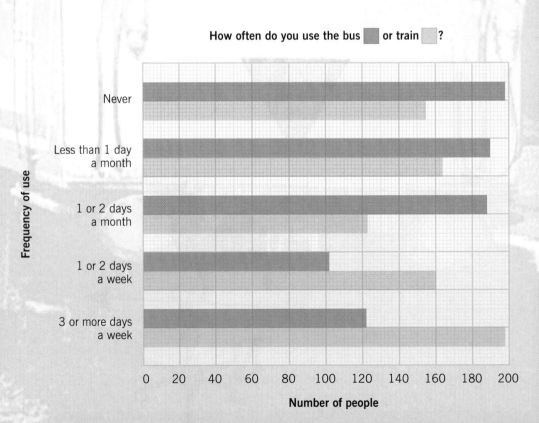

How often do you use the bus ▮ **or train** ▯ **?**

Frequency of use

Never

Less than 1 day a month

1 or 2 days a month

1 or 2 days a week

3 or more days a week

0 20 40 60 80 100 120 140 160 180 200

Number of people

Data Sheet Practice

You will need to use the data sheet for **Village bus and train services** to answer these questions.

(1) Which location for the new station has least support?

(2) What proportion of the 800 respondents:

   (a) are in favour of East Lane? Give your answer as a fraction.

   (b) gave no reply? Give your answer as a percentage.

(3) How many people use the bus?

(4) How many people use the train on '1 or 2 days a month'?

(5) How often do 160 people use the train?

(6) Pippa says that on '3 or more days a week' approximately 60% more people use the train than the bus.
Is she right?

(7) How often do 58 more people use the train than the bus?

(8) Give an approximate ratio of bus to train use for '1 or 2 days a month'.

(9) Of the people who use the train, what percentage travel by train at least once a week?

(10) Three people use two or three buses each to get to work.
The cost of their tickets is:

    Person A   £4.00
    Person B   £4.80
    Person C   £6.80

A Day Saver ticket for use on all buses is available for £3.50.
What is the percentage saving for each person?

Data Sheet Questions

You will need to use the data sheet for **Village bus and train services** to answer these questions.

1 What proportion of the people who returned surveys gave no answer to the question about location? *(1 mark)*

2 How many people who replied to the survey have no preference about the location? *(2 marks)*

3 Questions in the survey asked for:
   • An opinion about the location of the new train station.
   • How often the bus and train service is used.

Write another question that could have been included in the survey. Include a response section. *(2 marks)*

4 Show that 5% more of the people who replied to the survey never get the bus than never get the train. *(1 mark)*

5 What percentage of people use the train less than once a month? Give your answer to 1 d.p. *(2 marks)*

6 The 12 000 village population is likely to increase by 14% by 2010.

Use the results of the survey to give a rough estimate of the number of people in 2010 who are likely to use the train service at least once a week or more. *(3 marks)*

7 A journey to work by bus requires two maximum single rides.

Bus Fares	
Short hop (up to 2 fare stages)	£1.00
Maximum single ride	£1.40
Day Saver	£3.50
Evening Saver	£1.80

a What is the cost of the return journey to and from work using the maximum single rides? *(2 marks)*

b Work out the percentage saving that is made with a Day Saver ticket. *(2 marks)*

8 Give two possible reasons why any conclusions based on the replies to the survey might not be valid. *(2 marks)*

Extension Questions

① Is the data from the survey Primary Data or Secondary Data?
Explain your answer.

② Look at the graph 'How often do you use the bus or train?'
What is wrong with the choice of answers to the question?

Due to low response from the first survey, a second survey was sent to homes
that had not responded. The table below shows the results of the second survey.

How often do you use the bus or train?	Bus	Train
Never	261	170
Less than once a month	320	185
At least once but less than four times a month	113	148
At least once but less than three times a week	105	90
At least three times but less than five times a week	96	164
Five or more times a week	65	203

③ (a) Rewrite the results for trains in a grouped frequency table.

(b) In what class is the median number of train users?

(c) Calculate an estimate of the mean number of train users.

(d) Which average should train operators use to show that trains
are popular? Explain why.

④ Draw a histogram showing train users.

Something in the air

The fuel economy label shows the emission figures for carbon dioxide (CO_2).

The label shows ratings from band A (green) to band G (red).

The label shows a carbon dioxide emission of 175 g/km.

A carbon dioxide emission of 175 g/km puts the car in band E.

Fuel Economy

CO_2 emission figure (g/km)

<100	A
101-120	B
121-150	C
151-165	D
166-185	E
186-225	F
226+	G

E   175 g/km

1. What is the smallest carbon dioxide emission for a car in band E?   *(1 mark)*

2. Copy and complete this table.   *(3 marks)*

Make	Model	Fuel type	CO_2 emission (g/km)	Band
Fiat	Panda	Petrol	135	
Ford	Focus	Diesel	114	
Ford	Galaxy	Petrol	242	
Renault	Scenic	Diesel	136	
Smart	Coupe	Petrol	113	
Toyota	Hiace	Petrol	221	

The following table is used to work out how much vehicle tax you have to pay each year.

Vehicles registered on or after 1st March 2001					
Bands	CO_2 emission figure (g/km)	Diesel Car		Petrol Car	
		12 months rate £	6 months rate £	12 months rate £	6 months rate £
Band A	Up to 100	0.00	n/a	0.00	n/a
Band B	101 to 120	35.00	n/a	35.00	n/a
Band C	121 to 150	115.00	63.25	115.00	63.25
Band D	151 to 165	140.00	77.00	140.00	77.00
Band E	166 to 185	165.00	90.75	165.00	90.75
Band F	186 to 225	205.00	112.75	205.00	112.75
Band G	226+	300.00	165.00	300.00	165.00

3 What is the cost of 12 months' tax on a diesel car in band F? *(1 mark)*

4 What is the cost of 6 months' tax on a petrol car in band G? *(1 mark)*

5 Bill drives a Renault Scenic diesel.
What is the cost of 6 months' vehicle tax? *(1 mark)*

6 The emission figure (g/km) shows the number of grams of carbon dioxide per kilometre travelled.

The emission figure for a Volkswagen Passat is 182 g/km.
The car travels 520 km in one week.
How much carbon dioxide does the car emit?
Give your answer in kilograms to the nearest kilogram. *(3 marks)*

7 Last year Mr Smith drove a Toyota Hiace for 20 000 km.
Next year he plans to drive a Renault Scenic diesel.
He aims to halve his total CO_2 emissions from driving.
What is the maximum distance he can drive next year and still meet this target? *(3 marks)*

Extension Questions

1 On a journey of 30 km, the carbon dioxide emission of a car is measured as 6000 g.
Which band is the car most likely to be in?

2 The emission figure for a Porsche 911 is 266 g/km.
The car travels 160 miles in one day.
What is the emission of carbon dioxide?
Use the fact that 8 kilometres is approximately 5 miles.
(Give your answer in kilograms to the nearest kilogram).

3 The carbon dioxide emission of a car in band C is measured as 15 kg in one year. What is the minimum number of miles the car could have travelled in one year?

To smoke or not to smoke

Pre-release data sheet

Table 1: Percentage of adult smokers in the UK between 1974 and 2005

	Percentage of adult population in year								
	1974	1978	1982	1986	1990	1994	1998	2002	2005
Men	51	45	38	35	31	28	28	27	25
Women	41	37	33	31	29	26	26	25	23
All	45	40	35	33	30	27	27	26	24

Table 2: Cigarette smoking by age in the UK between 1978 and 2005

	Percentage of population aged					
	16 to 19	20 to 24	25 to 34	35 to 49	50 to 59	60+
1978	34	44	45	45	45	30
1988	28	37	36	36	33	23
1998	31	40	35	30	27	16
2000	29	35	35	29	27	16
2005	24	32	31	27	24	14

Table 3: Percentage of secondary school children who smoke – 1982 to 2006

	Percentage of boys and girls aged 15										
	1982	1986	1990	1992	1994	1996	1998	2000	2002	2005	2006
Boys	24	18	25	21	26	28	19	21	20	16	16
Girls	25	27	25	25	30	33	29	26	26	25	24
All	25	22	25	23	28	30	24	23	23	20	20

Tables 1–3 reproduced from 'Smoking Statistics: Who smokes and how much' produced by ASH. Crown copyright material is reproduced with the permission of the Controller of HMSO.

Data Sheet Practice

You will need to use the data sheet for **To smoke or not to smoke** to answer these questions.

Look at Table 1

1. In which 4-year period did smoking decrease the most?

2. In the same 4-year period did smoking decrease more with men or women?

Look at Table 2

3. Which age group has always smoked the least?

4. Has smoking decreased more with 20 to 24 year olds or with 25 to 34 year olds?

Look at Table 3

5. In 2006 did more 15-year-old boys smoke than 15-year-old girls?

6. What extra information would you need to work out the actual numbers of 15-year-old boys and girls smoking?

   Explain how you would do this.

'YOU'RE WELCOME SON'

www.CartoonStock.com

Data Sheet Questions

You will need to use the data sheet for **To smoke or not to smoke** to answer these questions.

1 **(a)** Describe the trend in the percentage number of adult smokers in the UK since 1994. *(2 marks)*

(b) A review of the future of the National Health Service concludes that for health reasons the percentage of adult smokers needs to reduce to 17% by 2011. Is this target likely to be reached?

Explain your answer. *(2 marks)*

2 In what age group did smoking decrease the **least** between 1978 and 2005?

Explain your answer. *(2 marks)*

3 In 2006 there were 403 000 boys aged 15 and 382 000 girls aged 15.

How many more girls than boys smoked in 2006? *(3 marks)*

4 There is a health warning in large black print on all packets of cigarettes. For example, on some packets the phrase **'Smoking kills'** is printed.

Here are some statistics from a Government publication that support this.

- It is estimated that in the UK smoking kills more than 13 people an hour.
- Out of every thousand people who start smoking when they are teenagers and continue to smoke 20 a day, one will be murdered, six will die in road accidents and **about 250 will be killed before their time by smoking**.
- On average, each cigarette shortens a smoker's life by around 11 minutes.

(a) Estimate how many people have died from smoking in the UK in the last 8 years. *(2 marks)*

Tina is 23 years old.
She has smoked 20 cigarettes a day every day for 8 years.

(b) If Tina continues to smoke 20 cigarettes a day, what is the probability that she will die before her time due to smoking? *(1 mark)*

(c) By how many weeks is she likely to have shortened her life in the last 8 years? *(3 marks)*

Extension Questions

Table 4: Daily consumption of manufactured cigarettes per smoker, 1979–2005

Year	Men	Women
1979	21.6	16.6
1990	16.8	13.9
2000	15	13
2002	15	13
2005	14	13

Table 4 reproduced from 'Smoking Statistics: Who smokes and how much' produced by ASH.
Crown copyright material is reproduced with the permission of the Controller of HMSO.

Table 5: Population of UK, 1979–2005 (to the nearest 1000)

Year	Men	Women
1979	27 236 000	28 432 000
1990	27 615 000	28 820 000
2000	28 385 000	29 382 000
2002	28 648 000	29 548 000
2005	29 127 000	29 906 000

1 **a** Use the information in **Tables 1**, **4** and **5** to copy and complete **Table 6**.
Give each value in the table to the nearest 1000.
You will need to estimate some of the values.

b Try to predict when the total number of cigarettes consumed by the adult population will be less than 100 million.

Table 6: Number of cigarettes consumed, 1979–2005

Year	Number of cigarettes (nearest 1000)	
	Men	Women
1979		
1990	143 819 000	
2000		97 401 000
2002		
2005		

Tables 5–6 from Census 2001 (National Statistics website: www.statistics.gov.uk).
Crown copyright material is reproduced with the permission of the Controller of HMSO.

Healthy workers

The table gives information about the number of healthcare workers and workers in other industries in England.

	Healthcare sector		Other industries		All industries (=100%)
	%	thousands	%	thousands	thousands
North East	7	74	93	936	1 010
North West	7	198	93	2 622	2 821
Yorkshire and the Humber	7	146	93	1 979	2 125
East Midlands	6	115	94	1 750	1 865
West Midlands	6	138	94	2 126	2 264
East of England	5	135	95	2 360	2 495
London	6	191	94	3 034	3 225
South East	6	214	94	3 540	3 754
South West	6	139	94	2 065	2 204

1   Which area has the highest number of healthcare workers? (*1 mark*)

2   Which area has the lowest percentage of healthcare workers? (*1 mark*)

3   There are 1 150 000 workers in Wales.
    8% of them work in the healthcare sector.
    How many workers in Wales work in the healthcare sector? (*2 marks*)

The graph shows the percentage of males and females employed as key healthcare workers in England and Wales.

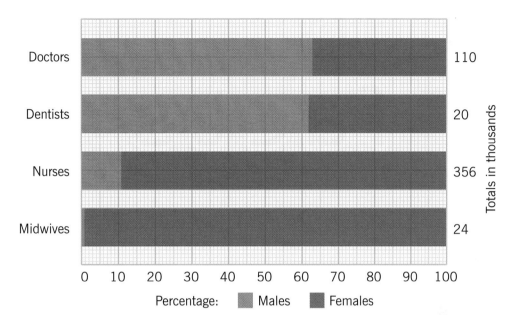

4 Work out the total number of key healthcare workers in England and Wales. *(2 marks)*

5 a Work out the percentage of nurses that are male. *(1 mark)*

b How many more female nurses are there than male nurses? *(3 marks)*

6 How many male key workers are employed in the healthcare sector in total? *(2 marks)*

7 How many female dentists are employed in the healthcare sector? *(2 marks)*

Extension Questions

1 There are 1 350 000 workers in the healthcare sector in England.
This represents 6% of the total number of workers.
Work out the total number of workers in England.

2 What percentage of workers in the key healthcare sector are male?

3 How many male midwives are employed in the healthcare sector?

4 The healthcare sector has 1 439 000 workers.
What percentage of the healthcare sector are male midwives?

Food facts

This information appears on a packet containing a quiche.

To oven heat (not frozen)
- pre-heat oven
- place on a baking tray

200°C 400°F Gas 6	20–25 mins

To oven heat from frozen
- pre-heat oven
- place on a baking tray

180°C 350°F Gas 4	35–40 mins

Nutritional information

Typical values	Per $\frac{1}{4}$ quiche as sold	Per 100 g as sold
Energy	262 calories	262 calories
Protein	6.9 g	6.9 g
Carbohydrate	19.9 g	19.9 g
Fat	17.2 g	17.2 g
Fibre	1.0 g	1.0 g
Sodium	0.40 g	0.40 g
Salt equivalent	1.0 g	1.0 g

Data Sheet Practice

You will need to use the data sheet for **Food facts** to answer these questions.

1. Polly takes her quiche out of the freezer and puts it in an electric oven.
   Her oven shows temperatures in Fahrenheit.
   What setting should she use?

2. Manesh has a quiche that is not frozen.
   He puts it in a pre-heated oven at 6:50 pm.
   At what time will the quiche be cooked?

3. How much protein is in 100 g of quiche?

4. How much fat is in 250 g of quiche?

5. What is the weight of a whole quiche?

6. The amount of fibre in 100 g of quiche is shown as 1.0 g.
   Is this rounded to the nearest whole number or to one decimal place?
   Explain your answer.

7. Damon is following a calorie-controlled diet and is aiming for an intake of 2000 calories per day.
   On Monday, he has 100 g of quiche for his breakfast and another 100 g for his lunch.
   How many more calories can he eat on Monday?

Data Sheet Questions

You will need to use the data sheet for **Food facts** to answer these questions.

(1) Paul's quiche is not frozen.
He has a gas oven.
What setting should Paul use to cook his quiche? *(1 mark)*

(2) Jane has a frozen quiche.
She wants to eat it at 1:15 pm.
At what time should she put it in the pre-heated oven? *(2 marks)*

(3) 3.3 g of the carbohydrate in the quiche is sugar.
Kate says, 'One sixth of the carbohydrate in this quiche is sugar.'
Is Kate correct?
You **must** show your working. *(2 marks)*

(4) How many calories are in 150 g of quiche? *(2 marks)*

(5) What percentage of the quiche is protein? *(1 mark)*

(6) The guideline daily amount of salt for adults is 6 g.

On Tuesday Joe eats $\frac{1}{3}$ of a quiche.
Joe does not want to eat more salt than the guideline daily amount.
How much more salt can Joe eat on Tuesday? *(4 marks)*

(7) The guideline daily amount of fat for an adult female is 70 g.
A 'Healthy Choice' chicken wrap contains 2.5 g of fat per 100 g.
One whole chicken wrap weighs 196 g.
Sara eats three chicken wraps.
Show that she has eaten more than 20% of the guideline daily amount of fat. *(4 marks)*

Extension Questions

1 Carbohydrate is approximately $\frac{1}{n}$ th of the content of the quiche, where n is an integer between 1 and 10.
Find the value of n.

2 Most values in the nutritional information have been rounded to one decimal place.
Which value given in grams has **not** been rounded to one decimal place?

3 **a** What is the maximum amount of salt in 200 g of quiche?

b What is the minimum amount of carbohydrate in one quiche?

4 The formula $F = \dfrac{9C}{5} + 32$ can be used to convert temperatures from Celsius to Fahrenheit.

a Make C the subject of the formula.

b Use your new formula to convert 350°F to Celsius.

c The quiche packet shows 180°C as equivalent to 350°F.
Calculate the percentage error in taking 180°C as the equivalent to 350°F.

To oven heat from frozen
- pre-heat oven
- place on a baking tray

180°C
350°F
Gas 4

35–40 mins

Lose those calories

Equipment	Rowing machine	Step machine	Exercise bike	Cross trainer	Running machine
Average calorie loss per minute	8	9	6	9	8

1. John eats a chocolate bar.
   The chocolate bar contains 375 calories.
   How many minutes does John have to exercise on the exercise bike to lose 375 calories? *(2 marks)*

2. Asif goes to the gym for half an hour.

   He spends $\frac{1}{3}$ of this time on the cross trainer.

   The rest of the time he spends on the running machine.
   How many calories does he lose? *(3 marks)*

3. On Wednesday Ben goes through this exercise programme:
   - 30 minutes on the exercise bike
   - 30 minutes on the cross trainer.

   On Thursday Ben decides to use **different** pieces of equipment.
   He wants to lose at least 10% more calories than he lost on Wednesday.
   Design an exercise programme for Ben to do this. *(4 marks)*

4. Gym equipment is set using a person's height and weight.
   The height and weight gives the **B**ody **M**ass **I**ndex (BMI).

   $$BMI = \frac{Weight\ (kg)}{Height^2\ (m)}$$

   Find the BMI for a person with a height of 175 cm and a weight of 56 kg. *(2 marks)*

Extension Questions

1 Kim exercises on the exercise bike, the cross trainer and the step machine.
- She spends twice the time on the cross trainer that she spends on the exercise bike.
- She spends half the time on the step machine that she spends on the exercise bike.

Calculate n, the amount of time she spends on the exercise bike if altogether Kim loses 285 calories.

2 For breakfast Michael had:
   50 g bacon
   25 g sausage
   150 g bread
   10 g butter
   black coffee with no sugar

Michael wants to lose 80% of the calories he eats for breakfast.
Design an exercise programme so that he can do this.

Calories per 100 g	
Bacon	400
Bread	220
Butter	740
Cornflakes	370
Sausages	184
Semi-skimmed milk (100 ml)	48
Sugar (1 teaspoon)	20
Tea or coffee (black)	0

3 Gym equipment is set using a person's height and weight.
The height and weight gives the **B**ody **M**ass **I**ndex (BMI).

$$\text{BMI} = \frac{\text{Weight (kg)}}{\text{Height}^2 \text{ (m)}}$$

a Chris's height is 180 cm. His weight is 93 kg. Work out his BMI.

This graph and table show how the Body Mass Index can be used to help decide if a person is overweight, normal weight or underweight.

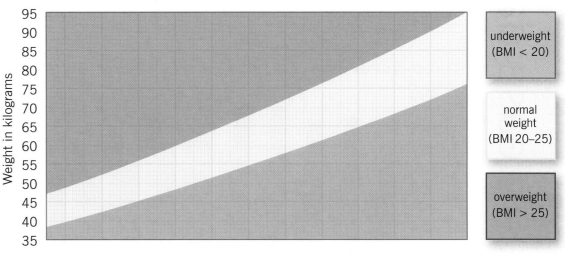

underweight (BMI < 20)

normal weight (BMI 20–25)

overweight (BMI > 25)

Weight in kilograms

Height in metres

b What percentage of his body weight must Chris lose for his BMI to be normal?

Deals on Wheels

Pre-release data sheet

Scooters for sale

This table shows the second-hand scooters for sale in a garage, Deals on Wheels.

Year	Make and model	Engine size cc	Mileage miles	Price £
2003	Italjet Jet-Set	125	19 155	595
2004	Piaggio Vespa	50	4 674	1 099
2006	Suzuki AY	50	2 000	1 499
2000	Aprilia Leonardo	250	3 278	1 295
2002	Gilera Runner	200	3 700	1 495
2003	Peugeot Elystar	125	2 000	695
2002	Yamaha Teos	125	4 600	1 499
2005	Vespa GT	200	450	2 399
2002	Peugeot Vivacity	100	8 608	599
2002	Piaggio NRG	50	3 055	650
2004	Yamaha CW	50	2 444	1 295
2005	Honda SCV	100	2 400	995
2006	Honda Lead	100	900	999
2004	Peugeot Speedfight	50	6 265	1 195
2001	Yamaha YP	125	28 661	1 195

This bar chart shows moped and motorcycle sales in Europe from 1994 to 2005.

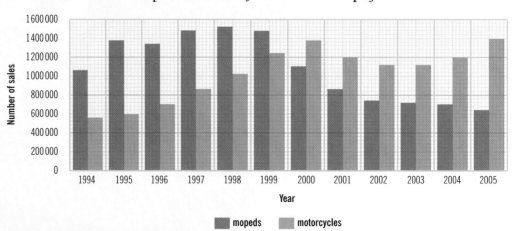

Data Sheet Practice

You will need to use the data sheet for **Deals on Wheels** to answer these questions.

1. Which is the oldest scooter?

2. Which scooter has done the least mileage?

3. What is the difference in price between the Yamaha Teos and the Honda SCV?

4. Lyndon wants to buy a scooter.
   - He wants the engine size to be less than 150 cc.
   - He wants the mileage to be less than 2500 miles.
   - He has up to £750 to spend.

   Which scooter should Lyndon buy?

5. Zoë is buying a scooter.
   - She wants a scooter made in 2003 or later.
   - She wants an engine size of 50 cc.
   - The mileage must be less than 2500 miles.
   - She doesn't want to spend more than £1300.

   Which scooter should Zoë buy?

6. (a) In which year were sales of motorcycles lowest?

   (b) How many were sold that year?

7. How many mopeds were sold in 1997?

8. How many more mopeds than motorcycles were sold in 1999?

9. What fraction of the scooters cost more than £1200? Write your fraction in its lowest terms.

10. What percentage of scooters were made in 2003 or later?

Data Sheet Questions

You will need to use the data sheet for **Deals on Wheels** to answer these questions.

1. Ben is buying a second-hand scooter from Deals on Wheels.
   - He wants a scooter made in 2004 or later.
   - It must have an engine size of at least 100 cc.
   - The mileage must be no more than 2000 miles.
   - The price must be less than £1000.

   Which scooter should Ben buy? *(2 marks)*

2. (a) The owner of Deals on Wheels keeps a record of his stock of scooters in a spreadsheet.

   Copy the spreadsheet and add the numbers for each type of scooter. *(3 marks)*

	A	B	C	D	E	F	G
1	Scooter stock						
2	**Engine size (cc)**	50	100	125	150	200	250
3	**Stock**	5					

   (b) Owners of scooters are charged vehicle tax based on the size of the engine.

   The garage owner wants to promote all the scooters that cost the least to tax.

   This table shows the cost of vehicle tax.

Cost of vehicle tax				
Size of engine (cc)	Not over 150	151–400	401–600	Over 600
Vehicle tax	£15	£32	£47	£47

   What proportion of scooters cost £15 for vehicle tax? *(2 marks)*

3. Kasim is buying a new scooter from Deals on Wheels for £3995.
   - He trades in his old scooter for £650 part exchange.
   - He pays a deposit of 20% of the amount he owes.

   How much is his deposit? *(3 marks)*

④ The owner of Deals on Wheels looks at the bar chart of moped and motorcycle sales in Europe from 1994 to 2005.

He uses the information to decide whether to sell mopeds, motorcycles or a mixture of both in the future.

a. In which year did sales of motorcycles exceed sales of mopeds for the first time? *(1 mark)*

b. In which year were combined sales of mopeds and motorcycles greatest? *(1 mark)*

c. Comment on the different trends in moped and motorcycle sales between 1994 and 2005. *(1 mark)*

d. The owner asks you to advise him about selling mopeds or motorcycles in the future.

What would you recommend?

Give a reason for your answer. *(2 marks)*

Extension Questions

① What was the percentage increase in sales of motorcycles from 2004 to 2005?

② From 1993 to 1994 sales of motorcycles increased by 5%.
How many motorcycles were sold in 1993?
Give your answer to three significant figures.

③ The table below shows the quarterly profits for Deals on Wheels for 2005 and 2006.

Deals on Wheels Quarterly Profits								
Year	2005				2006			
Quarter	1st	2nd	3rd	4th	1st	2nd	3rd	4th
Profit (£ thousand)	8.7	12.5	11.2	9.1	9.1	13.0	11.8	9.9

a. Use the information to calculate the four-point moving averages.

b. Show this information on a graph.

c. What can you say about the trend?

CHICKEN NIBBLERS

Chicken Nibblers

Small box of 6 nibblers	92p
Large box of 9 nibblers	128p
Family box of 20 nibblers	260p

Chicken nibblers can be bought in boxes of 6, 9, and 20 nibblers.

1 What is the cost of a box of 6 chicken nibblers? *(1 mark)*

2 What is the least cost for 18 chicken nibblers? *(2 marks)*

3 Work out the cost of three family boxes and two large boxes of chicken nibblers. *(2 marks)*

4 What is the cheapest way of buying 38 chicken nibblers? *(2 marks)*

5 What is the largest number of chicken nibblers that can be bought for £5.00? *(2 marks)*

6 Colleen says that it is not possible to buy exactly 16 chicken nibblers. Is she correct? Give a reason for your answer. *(2 marks)*

Extension Questions

1 Tristan is working out different ways to buy exactly 78 chicken nibblers.

He can says that you can buy 3 family boxes and 2 large boxes.

He shows the information in a table:

Family (20)	Large (9)	Small (6)	Total
3	2	0	78

Copy the table.

Complete the table to show two other ways in which Tristan can buy exactly 78 chicken nibblers

2 Lewis says that it is not possible to buy exactly 30 chicken nibblers.
Is he correct? Give a reason for your answer.

3 Natasha has worked out that it is possible to buy any number of chicken nibblers greater than 50.

What is the largest number of chicken nibblers that **cannot** be bought?

4 Find all the different numbers of chicken nibblers that **cannot** be bought?
Give reasons for your answers.

Investigate further.

COSY CARPETS

A superb range of carpets to enhance your home

*Wide range of fashionable colours,
all with stain-resistant finish*

Top quality wool mixture carpets in four widths

	Plain	*Berber*	*Light Pattern*
2-metres wide	£17.99 per metre length	£19.95 per metre length	£21.99 per metre length
3-metres wide	£25.49 per metre length	£27.79 per metre length	£29.99 per metre length
4-metres wide	£32.99 per metre length	£34.99 per metre length	£36.49 per metre length
5-metres wide	£38.99 per metre length	not available	£44.99 per metre length

Extend the life of your new carpet with our keenly priced underlay

Firmapad Underlay

Light or medium use   £3.95 per square metre

Heavy domestic use   £4.95 per square metre

Light use = bedroom, study
Medium use = dining room
Heavy domestic use = hall, stairs, living room

**We offer easy terms on all fitted carpets
– only 5% down and up to 3 years to pay the balance –**

Data Sheet Practice

You will need to use the data sheet for **Cosy carpets** to answer these questions.

1 Pete's bedroom is 3 metres wide and 2.5 metres long.

He wants to fit a plain carpet in the bedroom.

a What is the cost of 1 metre of 3-metre wide plain carpet?

b How much will it cost Pete to buy the carpet for the bedroom?

c Find the cost of underlay for Pete's bedroom.

2 Mr Beckham buys fitted carpets for the hall, stairs and landing of his new house.
  • The bill is £985.17
  • He pays 5% deposit, followed by 24 monthly payments of £58.95

How much extra does he pay?

3 This is the floor plan of Melissa's bedroom.

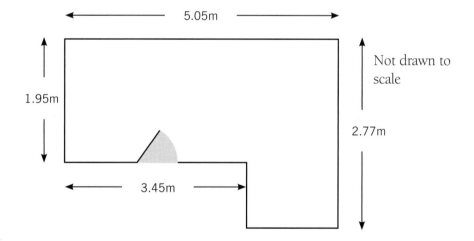

5.05m

Not drawn to scale

1.95m

2.77m

3.45m

GRIPPER RODS

42p per metre strip

a Which width of carpet would be most suitable for this bedroom? (You should assume that Melissa does not want any joins in the carpet).

b Find the cost of carpeting the bedroom with patterned carpet.

c Show that approximately 4 square metres of carpet will be wasted.

d Carpet grippers are used to fix the carpet. Grippers are placed around the perimeter of the room except for the doorway, which is 76 cm wide. How much will the gripper rods cost?

Data Sheet Questions

You will need to use the data sheet for **Cosy carpets** to answer these questions.

1 Shazia wants to buy Berber carpet for a bedroom that is 3 metres wide and 4 metres long.

  a What is the cheapest way she can do this?
  You **must** show your working. *(3 marks)*

  b Shazia also buys underlay for the bedroom.
  Calculate the cost of the underlay. *(2 marks)*

2 Dan buys fitted carpet and underlay for his flat.
  - The total price is £587.55.
  - He pays 5% deposit, followed by 36 monthly payments of £21.72.

  How much does he pay altogether? *(3 marks)*

3 The floor plan of Gary's living room is shown below.

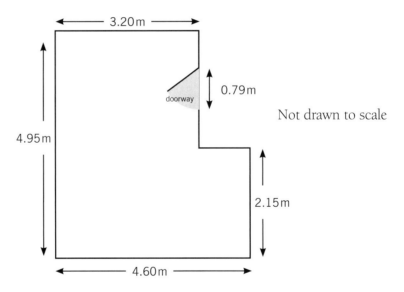

Not drawn to scale

Gary fits patterned carpet in his living room.

He chooses the cheapest way to do this without any joins.

  a How much does Gary pay for the carpet? *(2 marks)*

  b How much carpet is wasted? *(3 marks)*

  c Gary uses Tightgrip rods to fix the edge of the carpet.
  - Tightgrip rods are not used in doorways.
  - The doorway is 79 centimetres wide.

  How much does Gary pay for Tightgrip rods?
  Show your working. *(3 marks)*

TIGHTGRIP RODS

£4.25 per pack
(12 metre length)

Please note: we do not split the packs

Extension Questions

1 Marco buys carpet and underlay that costs £1250.

He chooses to pay 5% deposit and then £49.70 per month for 3 years.

Work out the percentage increase in the amount that Marco pays compared with the actual cost.

2 This is the floor plan of Jan's living room.

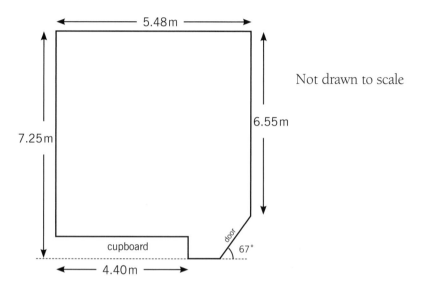

Not drawn to scale

a Jan buys plain carpet for this room.

She plans to have one join in the carpet.

Work out the cheapest way that Jan can carpet the room.

b The door opens back onto the wall beside the cupboard.

Is there enough space to open it right back against the wall?

Buying from a catalogue

Item	Price (£)
4GB MP3 player	129.00
Gents' classic quartz watch	26.99
All terrain skateboard	99.79
Street-X ramp combo (skateboard accessory)	89.99
Plush anti-bacterial pet duvet	17.99
Multi-function savings bank	24.99
Mini silver keyboard	29.99
Learn@Home keyboard skills	14.99
13MP USB webcam with microphone	24.99
Pro dartboard	24.99
Darts set	7.99
Table tennis balls	3.99
Table tennis bat	4.79
Art box set	14.99
Sudoku touch screen game	19.77

Sam makes this list of items he wants to buy from a catalogue.

[1] Sam chooses the skateboard and the skateboard accessory for his birthday.

How much do these items cost?   *(2 marks)*

[2] Sam's relatives give him a total of £200 for his birthday.

He decides to buy the MP3 player.

He then decides to buy the largest possible number of the other items that he can.

Write a list showing how Sam could spend his money.   *(2 marks)*

[3] Ben wants to buy a games console.

◀ He sees this entry in an online catalogue.

▼ This table shows the interest-free credit arrangements offered:

60GB Games console
+ 3 Games

£629.00

Extended Guarantee –
3 Years available for
£95.00

Time	Terms
20 weeks	Spread the cost of any item over 20 weeks interest-FREE
40 weeks	Spread the cost of any item of £59.99 or more over 40 weeks interest-FREE
50 weeks	Selected items and services are available over 50 weeks interest-FREE

Ben buys the games console and the 3-year extended guarantee.
He uses the 40 week interest-free credit arrangement.
A special offer means that Ben gets a 20% discount.

How much does he have to pay each week?   *(4 marks)*

Cash back
Cash back can be claimed in
these ways:
Goods
 For every £10 you pay, you
 can claim 15% cash back to
 purchase goods online.
A cheque
 For every £10 you pay, you
 can claim 12.5% cash back
 sent to you as a cheque.

4 The catalogue company operates a cash back scheme.

Ben completes the payments for the games console.

He then claims cash back in the form of a cheque.

Taking the cash back into account, how much does
Ben actually pay for the games console?   (*2 marks*)

Extension Questions

1 Anna buys three items from Sam's list.
 * She makes the purchases online.
 * She gets a 20% discount.
 * Anna pays for her purchases using 20 weeks interest-free credit.
 * She pays £2.59 per week.

What did Anna buy?

2 Tim has bought a HD Ready Digital LCD TV from the catalogue for £699.99.
 * He uses the cash back from this to help him buy a DVD recorder for £319.99.
 * He decides to order the DVD recorder online.
 * Tim gets a 20% discount.
 * He pays for the purchase using 40 weeks interest-free credit.

a How much does he pay each week?

After paying for the recorder, Tim claims cash back in the form of a cheque.

b How much cash back does he receive?

c How much does Tim actually pay for the recorder?

d What percentage is this of the original price?

3 Buying from a catalogue might not be the cheapest option even after discount and
cash back.

Use the internet to check prices from a variety of sources.

For example, choose a particular brand and model of TV.

Compare these internet prices with the price in a catalogue.

Don't forget:
 * To compare the real costs when buying by credit.
 * The costs of 'necessary' extras such as TV stands and guarantees.

Investigate further.

Garden design

Pre-release data sheet

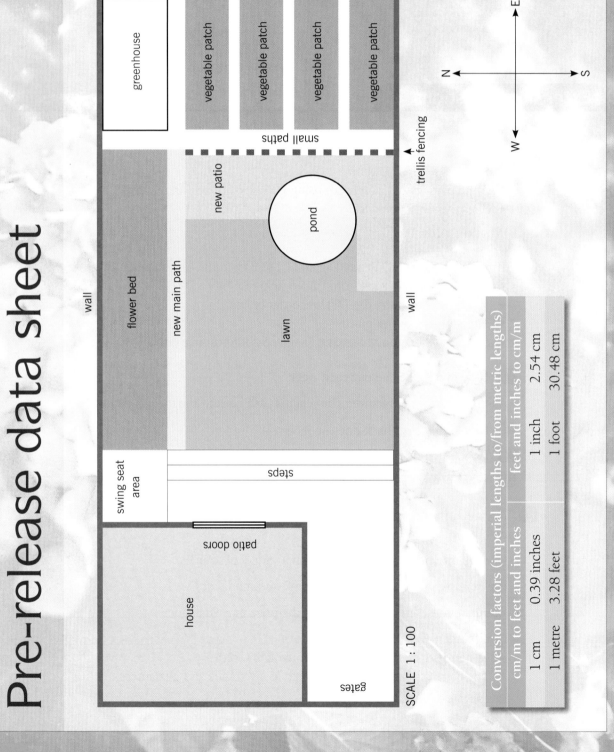

SCALE 1 : 100

Conversion factors (imperial lengths to/from metric lengths)		
cm/m to feet and inches	feet and inches to cm/m	
1 cm	0.39 inches	1 inch	2.54 cm
1 metre	3.28 feet	1 foot	30.48 cm

Data Sheet Practice

You will need to use the data sheet for **Garden design** to answer these questions.

1 **(a)** Measure the length and width of the greenhouse on the plan.

    (b) Ken says the real width of the greenhouse is over $1\frac{1}{2}$ metres. Show that he is right.

2   The pond will be edged with small bricks.

    (a) Find the circumference of the pond. (Use $\pi = 3.14$)

    (b) Assuming that the bricks are square with sides equal to 10 cm, work out the number of bricks needed to edge the pond.

    (c) Assuming that bricks are sold only in packs of 10, work out how many packs of bricks are required.

    (d) Work out the cost of the bricks at £19.99 per pack.

3 **(a)** What is the length of the trellis fence on the plan?

    (b) What is the real length of the trellis fence?

    (c) Trellis fencing is measured in feet (ft). Work out the length of the trellis fence in feet.

    (d) The shortest fence panels are 1 ft in length. What length of fencing will be bought?

Trellis fencing costs	
6 ft × 6 ft	£25.49
6 ft × 5 ft	£22.99
6 ft × 4 ft	£20.49
6 ft × 3 ft	£17.99
6 ft × 2 ft	£15.49
6 ft × 1 ft	£12.99

    (e) Use the table above to find the cost of the trellis fence.

4   The new patio is to be made using crazy paving.
Assuming that the builder charges £8 per square metre for crazy paving, work out the cost of the new patio.

Data Sheet Questions

You will need to use the data sheet for **Garden design** to answer these questions.

1 What is the actual length of the 'new main path'? *(1 mark)*

2 The diagram shows a wall planned to be built around the perimeter of the flower bed. Topsoil is going to be added to raise the level of the soil in the flower bed by 30 cm.

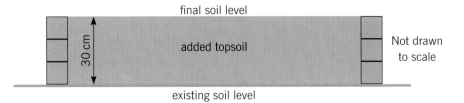

Topsoil is supplied in bags containing half a cubic metre.
How many bags are required to raise the level of the flower bed?

(3 marks)

3 The 'new main path' is to be paved with square paving slabs.
  - The length of each side of the slab is 50 cm.
  - The width of the 'new main path' is also 50 cm.
  - The slabs cost £6.99 each.
How much does it cost to pave the 'new main path'? *(3 marks)*

4 Sue wants to buy the longest swing seat that will fit in the position shown on the plan.

Three swing seats are advertised for sale in the local paper. Details of sizes and prices are shown below.

	Length	Cost
Swing seat 1	6 ft 6 in	£50
Swing seat 2	1.5 m	£55
Swing seat 3	6 ft 2 in	£50

Which seat does Sue buy? *(5 marks)*
You **must** show your working.

5 The lawn is to be planted with grass seed.
What is the area of the lawn?
Do **not** include the pond area. *(6 marks)*

Extension Questions

The tables show some information about the price of paving slabs which are sold in boxes of 10.

	Greenwich	Welford	Barnett
6 cm by 5 cm	£3.49 per box	£3.79	£3.19
8 cm by 5 cm	£3.79 per box	£3.99	£3.24
10 cm by 5 cm	£3.99 per box	£4.19	£3.49

Special offers	
Greenwich	**Welford (discount per box)**
10% off orders over £100	50p off 6 cm by 5 cm slabs
	50p off 8 cm by 5 cm slabs
	£1 off 10 cm by 5 cm slabs

1   Find the cheapest way of paving the small paths.

2   A tree is to be planted on the lawn.
The tree needs to be planted at least 1 metre from the wall, steps, path, patio and pond.

Make a tracing of the area marked 'lawn' on the plan, and mark (on the tracing) the area where the tree can be planted.

3   Ken wants to know that it is safe to have the steps as shown on the plan.
He does not want the steps to be under the area covered when the seat swings.

The swing seat is placed against the brick wall so that it faces south.
- The seat hangs on a split chain so that it can swing on a horizontal.
- The perpendicular height from the floor to the top of the chain is 6 ft.
- The seat is 2 ft above the floor.
- The seat swings up to 30° each side of the perpendicular.

a   Find *a* (in cm) the distance covered by the swing of the seat in a forwards direction.

b   Can the seat swing between the steps and the brick wall?
Explain your answer.

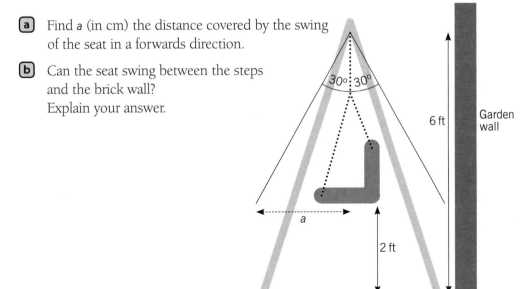

Get your skates on

A local council are improving a skate park.

1 They decide to paint one of the walls in the skate park.
The area of the wall is 45 m².
One litre of paint covers 12 m².

How many litres of paint are needed to paint the wall?   *(2 marks)*

2 The ramps in the skate park are to be replaced.
The diagram shows a sketch of a support for one of the
proposed ramps.

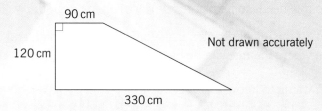

Each support is to be made of moisture-resistant MDF (medium
density fibreboard).

This is sold in rectangular sheets 2440 mm long and
1220 mm wide.

a Draw a sheet of MDF using a scale of 1 to 20.   *(2 marks)*

b On your scale drawing show how the sheet of MDF must
be cut to make one of the supports.

Shade the piece of MDF that is not used.   *(3 marks)*

3 The supports are to be painted orange.

The painters have some red and yellow paint.

To make orange paint they mix 13 parts of yellow paint with
7 parts of red.

The painters measure the paint they need using 200 ml tins.

They estimate that they need 8 litres of orange paint.

How many 200 ml tins of yellow paint are needed?

How many 200 ml tins of red paint are needed?   *(3 marks)*

Extension Questions

There is a children's playground next to the skate park.
The leftover paint is used to redecorate some of the equipment in the playground.

1   There are two climbing walls in the playground.
They are **similar** shapes.
The small wall is 2 metres wide.
The large wall is 3 metres wide.
It takes 600 ml to paint the smaller wall.

How much paint will the large wall need?

2   The side of the rocker under the seesaw in the
playground is a segment of the quadrant *AOB* shown
shaded in the diagram.

The curved length, *AB*, is 2.5 metres.

a   Find the radius of the quadrant. (Use $\pi = 3.14$)

b   Work out the area of the segment that needs to
be painted. (Use $\pi = 3.14$)

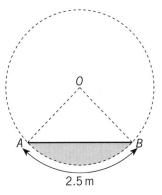

2.5 m

3   The base of the roundabout is a frustum of a cone.
- The radius of the top is 25 cm.
- The radius of the base is 50 cm.
- The slant height of the frustum is 60 cm.

a   Let the length of the slant height of the cut-off cone
be *x* cm. Using similar triangles, find *x*.

b   Find the area of the curved surface of the frustum.
(Use $\pi = 3.14$)

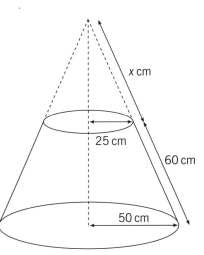

x cm

25 cm

60 cm

50 cm

Fish tanks

The photographs below show two species of goldfish that are commonly kept as pets.

Lionhead goldfish
Fish body area = 12 cm^2

Common goldfish
Fish body area = 8 cm^2

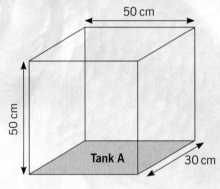

50 cm

50 cm

Tank A

30 cm

Fish tanks are nearly always prisms. The diagrams here show three different cuboid-shaped fish tanks.

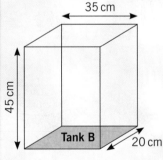

35 cm

45 cm

Tank B

20 cm

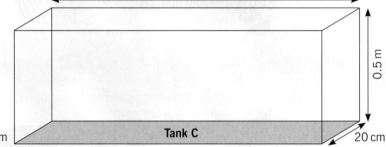

1.4 m

0.5 m

Tank C

20 cm

A tank can accommodate a limited amount of fish depending on the area of the water surface. This is because the water surface is important for the exchange of gases such as oxygen and carbon dioxide, which are essential for the fish to survive.

Guide for the maximum area of fish to have in a tank

Area of the water surface (cm^2)	Area of fish body (cm^2)
100	10
150	15
1000	100
1500	150

Data Sheet Practice

You will need to use the data sheet for **Fish tanks** to answer these questions.

1 **a** What is the perimeter of the base of tank B?

b What is the perimeter of the base of tank C?

2 **a** Work out the area of the water surface in tank A.

Look at the table: Guide for the maximum area of fish to have in a tank.

b Work out the maximum area of fish that tank A should hold.

c What is the maximum number of lionhead goldfish that can be put in tank A?

3 **a** Work out the area of the water surface in tank C.

b Work out the maximum area of fish that tank C should hold.

c What is the maximum number of common goldfish that can be put in tank C?

4 Tank C is filled to the top with water. What is the volume of water in the tank?

Give your answer in cubic centimetres.

5 The cross-section of three fish tanks are shown.

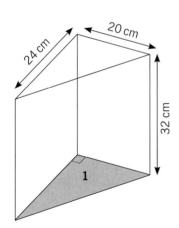

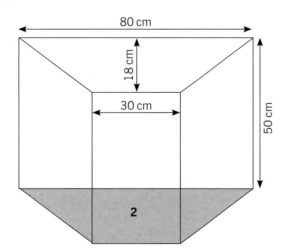

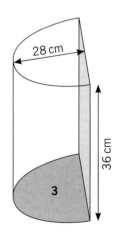

a Work out the perimeter of the base of the triangular tank.

b Work out the maximum number of common goldfish that the trapezium-based tank (tank 2) can hold.

c Work out the total edge length of the semicircular tank. (Use π = 3.14)

Data Sheet Questions

You will need to use the data sheet for **Fish tanks** to answer these questions.

1 A plastic seal is put around the base of tank A.
Work out the length of seal that is needed. *(2 marks)*

2 **a** Work out the area of the water surface in tank B.
Give your answer in square centimetres. *(2 marks)*

b Lionhead goldfish cost £4.60 each.
Work out the cost of putting the maximum possible number of lionhead goldfish in tank B. *(4 marks)*

3 Tank A is filled with water up to 5 cm from the top of the tank.
Tank B is filled with water up to 2 cm from the top of the tank.
How much more water does tank A hold than tank B?
Give your answer in cubic centimetres. *(3 marks)*

4 There are 133 litres of water in tank C.
How deep is the water in tank C? *(3 marks)*

5 The cross-section of a fish tank is made up of a rectangle and a semicircle.

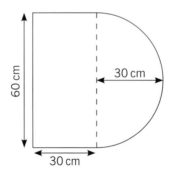

The fish tank is 38 cm high.
The tank is filled with water up to 3 cm from the top of the tank.
15% of the water is changed each week.
How much water is changed each week? (Use $\pi = 3.14$)
Give your answer in litres. *(5 marks)*

Extension Questions

Tropical fish need to be kept in warm water.

This means that the water in the tank needs to be heated.

The size of the heater required, measured in watts, depends on the volume of the water.

Size of heater (watts)	Capacity of tank (litres)
50	Up to 27 litres
100	27 to 54 litres
150	54 to 81 litres

1 Each of these tanks is filled to the top.

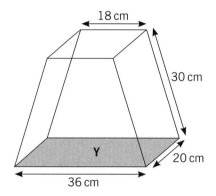

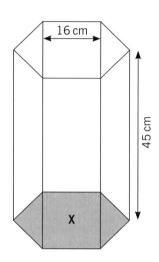

a Find the volume of water in (i) tank X (ii) tank Y.
(Give your answers in cubic centimetres.)

b Give the size of heater required for (i) tank X (ii) tank Y.

2 Some tanks are sub-divided into sections so that different fish can be kept in the same tank.

A large cylindrical tank is in the middle of a shop.

- The diameter of the tank is 1.8 m.
- The height of the tank is 0.8 m.
- The water level in the tank is 10 cm below the top of the tank.
- A triangular frame is put in the tank dividing it into three sections.
- The centre of the circle, **O**, is a vertex of the triangle.

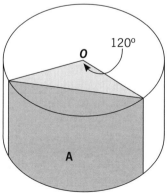

The diagram shows the tank and the triangular frame.

What is the volume (in litres) of:

a water in the triangular section of the tank?

b water in section A of the tank? (Use $\pi = 3.14$)

Popular TV

An advertiser studies a report about TV viewing to help decide which channel to use for an advert.

1 **a** What was ITV1's percentage share of the viewing in 2005? *(1 mark)*

b Describe what happened to each channel's share of the viewing between 1997 and 2006. *(3 marks)*

2 **a** Tom says that in 2006 ITV1's share of the commercial channel's viewing was $\frac{1}{5}$
Is Tom right?
Give a reason for your answer. *(1 mark)*

b The average time a person spent watching TV in 2006 was 28 hours per week.

Estimate the average time per week a person spent watching Channel 5 in 2006.
Give your answer in hours correct to 1 decimal place. *(3 marks)*

3 'Deal or No Deal' is a game show on Channel 4. The table gives its Sunday and Monday viewing figures over a five-week period.

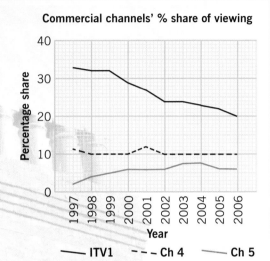

Commercial channels' % share of viewing

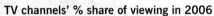

— ITV1   – – Ch 4   — Ch 5

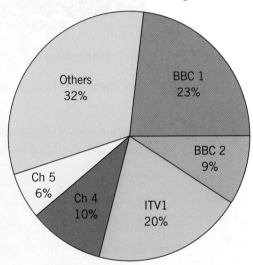

TV channels' % share of viewing in 2006

Others 32%
BBC 1 23%
BBC 2 9%
ITV1 20%
Ch 4 10%
Ch 5 6%

Week	1	2	3	4	5	Total
Sunday	3.28	2.62	3.13	3.54	3.57	16.14
Monday	4.01	3.94	3.59	3.75	3.49	18.78

	Sunday	Monday
Mean		3.756 million
Range		0.52 million

a Calculate the mean and range for Sunday's viewing figures over the same period. Complete the table. *(2 marks)*

b Which of these days do you think the advertiser should choose to show the advert?
Explain your answer. *(2 marks)*

Extension Questions

1 **a** Write the viewing shares for ITV1 and Channel 4 in 2006 as a simplified ratio.

b Explain what your answer to part (a) tells you.

2 **a** Write BBC1 and BBC2's total share of the viewing in 2006 as a fraction in its simplest terms.

b Use your answer to part (a) to estimate the probability that someone watching TV in 2006 is not watching BBC1 or BBC2.

3 **a** Find the median viewing figure for each day using the table on page 52.

b Explain why the mean is a better average to use for the viewing figures than either the median or the mode.

c What else might an advertiser consider when deciding where to show an advert? List your ideas.

4 The table gives estimates for the adult population of the UK. All figures are in thousands, to the nearest thousand.

Age	Male	Female
18–24	2794	2697
25–44	8512	8630
45–64	7265	7503
65 and over	4143	5505

A market research company wants to send a questionnaire about television to 5000 adults.

Calculate the number of questionnaires they should send to each category to give a stratified sample.

PETROL STATION

Asim is the manager of a petrol station that also contains a small shop. The petrol station usually closes at 8 pm but stays open until 10 pm on Friday night. Asim wants to investigate whether it is worth the petrol station staying open as late as it does.

The following information was collected over a period of 2 hours on a Friday night. He collects information on types of vehicles, ages of vehicles, fuel costs and other purchases as well as the time spent at the petrol station.

Vehicle	Age (years)	Fuel costs	Other costs	Time (mins)
Car	2	£22.00	£6.20	9
Motorbike	3	£15.50	£1.20	7
Car	1	£26.00	£2.80	4
Motorbike	2	£12.00	£0.85	5
Car	11	£13.00	£4.15	6
Lorry	4	£38.00	£22.90	16
Car	1	£23.00	£7.15	10
Car	2	£24.50	£6.05	11
Car	1	£28.00	£3.45	13
Lorry	2	£34.00	£13.90	13
Car		£27.50		11
Lorry	8	£34.00	£15.60	14
Car	1	£7.00		4
Motorbike	1	£7.50		4
Car	1	£10.00	£2.20	5
Motorbike	1	£11.00	£3.00	6
Car	5	£15.00	£4.65	7
Lorry	3	£26.50	£11.30	12
Car	3	£18.50	£3.85	8
Car	1	£22.00	£5.15	9

Data Sheet Practice

You will need to use the data sheet for **Petrol station** to answer these questions.

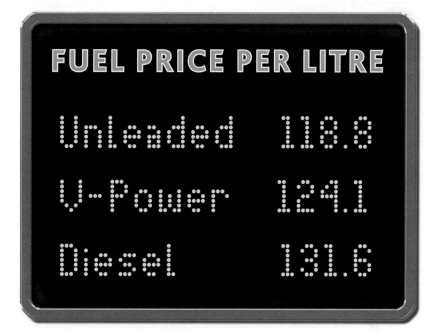

FUEL PRICE PER LITRE

Unleaded 118.8

V-Power 124.1

Diesel 131.6

(1) What is the cost of 10 litres of unleaded petrol?

(2) What is the cost of 20 litres of diesel?

(3) How many vehicles were sampled during the survey?

(4) How many motorbikes and lorries were sampled?

(5) Work out the total amount of money spent on fuel.

(6) What items might be included under 'Other costs'?

(7) Work out the total amount of money spent on car fuel and state this as a percentage of total fuel costs.

(8) What is the median, mode and range of the ages of the vehicles?

Data Sheet Questions

You will need to use the data sheet for **Petrol station** to answer these questions.

1. How many cars were sampled during the survey? *(1 mark)*

2. Work out the total amount of money spent on other costs. *(2 marks)*

3. Draw and label a suitable diagram to show the different types of vehicle at the petrol station. *(3 marks)*

4. (a) Work out the average time spent at the petrol station between 8 pm and 10 pm on Friday.

   (b) Between 6 pm and 8 pm on Friday the average amount of time spent at the petrol station was 7.5 minutes.

   Compare the times spent at the petrol station on Friday between 6 pm and 8 pm and between 8 pm and 10 pm. *(3 marks)*

5. Asim thinks there is a relationship between the fuel cost and time spent at the petrol station.
   Draw a scatter graph to investigate whether this is true.
   Comment on the relationship. *(4 marks)*

6. One of the items of data seems incorrect.
   Draw a line of best fit on your scatter graph.
   Use your line of best fit to suggest a better value. *(2 marks)*

Extension Questions

(1) One of the data items is missing. Give a possible reason for this.

(2) Calculate the mean age of the cars at the petrol station.
Give your answer to an appropriate degree of accuracy.

(3) Asim thinks there is a relationship between the other costs and time
spent at the petrol station.
Complete a scatter graph and comment on the relationship.

(4) Calculate the total amount of income at the petrol station during the survey.

(5) Explain why this amount might not reflect the true income at the petrol station.

Speed watch

Typical Stopping Distances

Speed	Thinking distance	Braking distance	Stopping distance
20 mph	6 metres	6 metres	12 metres (40 feet) or 3 car lengths
30 mph	9 metres	14 metres	23 metres (75 feet) or 6 car lengths
40 mph	12 metres	24 metres	36 metres (120 feet) or 9 car lengths
50 mph	15 metres	38 metres	53 metres (175 feet) or 13 car lengths
60 mph	18 metres	55 metres	73 metres (240 feet) or 18 car lengths
70 mph	21 metres	75 metres	96 metres (315 feet) or 24 car lengths

Source: The Highway Code

In wet weather, stopping distances will be at least double those required for stopping on dry roads.

1. (a) What is the stopping distance at 30 mph in dry conditions?
Compare this with the stopping distance at 20 mph in wet conditions. *(2 marks)*

    (b) Advice for driving in wet conditions is that speed should be reduced by one third.
Explain how your answer to part (a) supports this advice. *(1 mark)*

2. Anya says that the braking distance is twice the thinking distance.
Explain why she is wrong. *(1 mark)*

3. Jodie is driving at 40 mph.
    • The roads are wet.
    • She sees a fallen tree in the road 200 feet ahead of her.
Will she be able to stop in time? Explain your answer. *(2 marks)*

4. The formula connecting thinking distance, T, to the speed, V, is $T = \frac{3V}{10}$
Write down one example to show that this is true. *(1 mark)*

5. The speed limit on a single carriageway road is 60 mph.
Tim and Bill are both travelling on the road in **wet** conditions.
Tim is travelling at 10 mph **above** the speed limit.
Bill is travelling at 10 mph **below** the speed limit.
They both see a hazard at the moment that Tim overtakes Bill.
They apply the brakes on their vehicles at the same time.
How much further than Bill does Tim travel before his vehicle stops? *(4 marks)*

Extension Questions

1. Todd says that one car length is equal to 4 metres.

    a Analyse the stopping distance data to check Todd's statement.

    b Why has the variation occurred?

2. Kate says that the typical stopping distance in car lengths, C, is given by the formula:

    $$C = \frac{3V}{10} - 3 \text{ where } V \text{ is the speed.}$$

    Test Kate's formula.
    Is it always true, sometimes true or never true?

3. **a** Plot the typical stopping distance, d metres, against the speed, V mph.
    Join your points with a smooth curve.

    b Use your graph to estimate the stopping distance at a speed of 45 mph.

    c Describe how the gradient of the graph changes as the speed increases.

    d Jo thinks the equation of the curve is of the form $d = aV^2 + bV + c$.
    Investigate.

Trips on Tyneside

Pre-release data sheet

Part of the timetable for a South Shields bus is given below.

Low Moorsley	0803	–	0833	–	0903	then at	03	–	33	–	1503	–	1533	–	1603	–	1633
Hetton-le-Hole	0809	0831	0839	0901	0909	these	09	31	39	01	1509	1531	1539	1601	1609	1631	1639
Houghton-le-Spring	0823	0838	0853	0908	0923	minutes	23	38	53	08	1523	1538	1553	1608	1623	1638	1653
Herrington Burn	0833	0848	0903	0918	0933	past	33	48	03	18	1533	1548	1603	1618	1633	1648	1703
Royal Hospital	0850	0905	0920	0935	0950	each	50	05	20	35 (until)	1550	1605	1620	1635	1650	1705	1720
Sunderland	0900	0915	0930	0945	1000	hour	00	15	30	45	1600	1615	1630	1645	1700	1715	1730
Cleadon	0917	0932	0947	1002	1017		17	32	47	02	1617	1632	1647	1702	1717	1732	1747
South Shields	0933	0948	1003	1018	1033		33	48	03	18	1633	1648	1703	1718	1733	1748	1803
South Shields	0852	0907	0922	0937	0952	then at	07	22	37	52	1507	1522	1537	1552	1607	1622	1637
Cleadon	0909	0924	0939	0954	1009	these	24	39	54	09	1524	1539	1554	1609	1624	1639	1654
Sunderland	0931	0946	1001	1016	1031	minutes	46	01	16	31	1546	1601	1616	1631	1646	1701	1716
Royal Hospital	0938	0953	1008	1023	1038	past	53	08	23	38 (until)	1553	1608	1623	1638	1653	1708	1723
Herrington Burn	0956	1011	1026	1041	1056	each	11	26	41	56	1611	1626	1641	1656	1711	1726	1741
Houghton-le-Spring	1006	1021	1036	1051	1106	hour	21	36	51	06	1621	1636	1651	1706	1721	1736	1751
Hetton-le-Hole	1023	1038	1053	1108	1123		38	53	08	23	1638	1653	1708	1723	1738	1753	1757
Low Moorsley	1029	–	1059	–	1129		29	–	59	–	1629	–	1659	–	1729	–	1759

The bus stops in South Shields at the market place where an open-air market is held every Monday and Saturday. It is a 5 minute walk from this bus stop to the Shields Ferry, which crosses the River Tyne between North Shields and South Shields.

Shields Ferry Timetable

Ferry	Times between 7 am and 8:07 pm
Departs North Shields	00 and 30 minutes past each hour
Arrives South Shields	07 and 37 minutes past each hour
Departs South Shields	15 and 45 minutes past each hour
Arrives North Shields	22 and 52 minutes past each hour

The Shields Ferry takes 7 minutes to cross the River Tyne.

Data Sheet Practice

You will need to use the data sheet for **Trips on Tyneside** to answer these questions.

1. A shopper wants to travel from Houghton-le-Spring to Sunderland.
   He reaches the Houghton-le-Spring bus stop at 9:20 am.

   a. What time is the next bus to Sunderland?

   b. How long does he have to wait?

   c. When will he arrive in Sunderland?

   d. How long does the journey take?

2. A Sunderland supporter lives at Hetton-le-Hole.
   He wants to catch the bus that arrives in Sunderland at 2:30 pm.

   a. What time does this bus leave Hetton-le-Hole?

   b. How long does the journey take?

3. A nurse lives at Low Moorsley and works at the Royal Hospital.

   a. How often is there a bus from Low Moorsley?

   b. The nurse starts work at 4:45 pm.
   Which is the latest bus she can catch?

   c. What time does this bus arrive at the hospital?

   d. How long is this before she starts work?

4. Ben lives in South Shields.
   He wants to visit a patient at the Royal Hospital.

   a. Afternoon visiting time starts at 2 o'clock.
   What is the latest bus he can catch from South Shields
   to get to the hospital before the start of visiting time?

   b. Ben stays until the end of visiting time at 3 o'clock.
   What is the earliest time he can get back to South Shields?

5. A woman from Cleadon has arranged to meet a friend for
   lunch at North Shields at 12:30 pm.

   a. What is the latest ferry she can catch from South Shields?

   b. What is the latest bus she can catch from Cleadon?

   c. How long will the journey take altogether?

   d. The friends finish lunch at ten minutes past two.
   What time is the next ferry to South Shields?

Data Sheet Questions

You will need to use the data sheet for **Trips on Tyneside** to answer these questions.

1 How often is there a bus from Herrington Burn to South Shields?

(2 marks)

2 Rachel travels from Low Moorsley to South Shields.
She wants to arrive before 5 o'clock in the afternoon.
What is the latest bus she can catch from Low Moorsley? *(2 marks)*

3 Carol catches the 1245 bus from Sunderland to South Shields.
At South Shields she takes the next ferry to North Shields.
The bus and ferry both run on time.
At what time does she arrive at North Shields? *(3 marks)*

4 Tom lives a few minutes from the bus station at Houghton–le–Spring.
He plans to visit the Fish Quay Festival in North Shields.
He wants to spend about 3 hours at the Festival and be home before 5.30 pm.
He decides to travel by bus and ferry.
Give full details of how he might do this. *(3 marks)*

The table below gives ticket prices for adults who travel on the Shields Ferry.

Ferry tickets	Conditions	Price
Single	Single journey in either direction	£1.00
Return	For a return journey	£1.95
7-day pass	Unlimited ferry travel during any 7 day period	£7.45
Book of tickets	Book of 10 single tickets – can be used on any day of the year	£9.00

This table gives bus fares between Cleadon and South Shields and special tickets that include the ferry to North Shields.

Bus tickets	Conditions	Price
Cleadon to South Shields	Single journey in either direction	70p
Cleadon to South Shields	For a return journey	£1.30
Transfare	One-way journey that includes bus and ferry	£1.40
Day Rover	Unlimited travel for one day including bus and ferry	£5.20

5 Sunita want to make one return journey from Cleadon to North Shields.
What is the cheapest way she can make this journey? *(2 marks)*

6 Tim lives in South Shields.
  • He has a holiday job in North Shields.
  • He expects to work there for six days each week for four weeks.
Which ferry tickets should he buy to keep his travel costs to a minimum?
You **must** show your working. *(3 marks)*

Extension Questions

1 How many buses go from Cleadon to South Shields between 10 am and 4 pm?

2 One day a crewmember works from 7 am until 12:22 pm on the ferry.
How many times does he cross the Tyne?

3 The travel graph models Jack's journey from the bus stop at Cleadon to the North Shields Fish Quay.

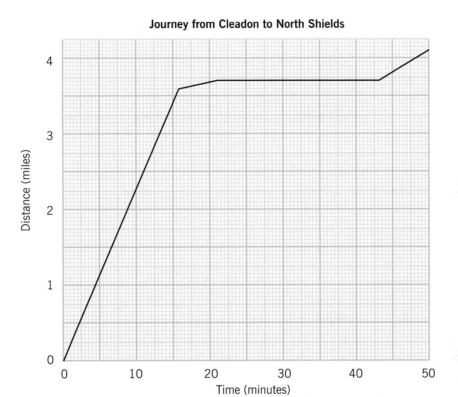

Journey from Cleadon to North Shields

a (i) How far does Jack travel on the bus?
(ii) Find the speed of the bus in miles per hour.

b How long does Jack wait for the ferry?

c Find the speed of the ferry in miles per hour.

d In what ways is the graph not an accurate model of Jack's journey?

e Explain how Jack could save some time on his journey.

4 A report on transport says that there is a probability of 0.95 that the bus to South Shields runs on time and a probability of 0.99 that the Shields Ferry sails on time.
Jane plans a journey on the bus and ferry. Calculate the probability that:

a both the bus and ferry are on time

b neither the bus nor the ferry are on time.

High fliers

The table gives the times for an airline's flights between Heathrow and Prague.

	Heathrow to Prague			Prague to Heathrow		
Departs	0840	1500	1820	0755	1240	1850
Arrives	1145	1755	2115	0910	1345	2000

1 a At what time is the morning flight from Prague due to arrive at Heathrow? *(1 mark)*

b On Tuesday the flight from Prague didn't arrive until 1205. How late was the plane on Tuesday? *(2 marks)*

2 The time in Prague is one hour ahead of the time at Heathrow. The 0840 flight from Heathrow to Prague leaves and arrives on time. How long does the flight actually take? *(2 marks)*

3 The airline records the delays on flights that travel from Heathrow to Prague during a bank holiday weekend. The table gives their results.

Delays in minutes on flights from Heathrow to Prague

Flight	0840	1500	1820
Saturday	5	15	30
Sunday	10	28	47
Monday	15	24	33

a What was the delay on the flight that left Heathrow at 3 pm on Monday? *(1 mark)*

b The mean delay for flights from Prague to Heathrow was 18 minutes.
The range was 54 minutes.
Use these values to compare the flight delays from Prague to Heathrow with those from Heathrow to Prague. *(6 marks)*

Extension Questions

The table gives the delays
(to the nearest minute)
for one year's flights from
Heathrow to Prague.
Early flights are counted
as a zero delay.

Delay (minutes)	% of flights
0–15	63
16–30	16
31–60	11
61–180	10
Over 180	0

1 Use the data in the table to estimate the probability that a flight from Heathrow to Prague will be over half an hour late.

2 a Estimate the mean value of the data given in the table.

b Why should this value not be used to find an estimate of the time of arrival of a flight from Heathrow to Prague?

3 The diagram shows a cumulative percentage graph of the data from question 1.

Delays on flights from Heathrow to Prague

Use the graph to estimate

a the median

b the interquartile range

c the percentage of flights that were delayed by over 45 minutes.

4 a Draw a histogram to illustrate the delay times.

b Describe what your histogram tells you about likely delay times for flights from Heathrow to Prague.

By the left, quick march

Groups of army cadets go on cross-country expeditions.

The time that expeditions take is estimated using Naismith's formula and Tranter's corrections.

Naismith's formula is used to estimate the time that a mountain walk will take.

Naismith's formula:　$t = 12d + \dfrac{h}{10}$
t is the time taken in minutes
d is the distance walked in kilometres
h is the height climbed or descended in metres

Tranter developed the following table of corrections to Naismith's formula.

Tranter's corrections make adjustments for fitness and fatigue. An individual's fitness is found by measuring the time he/she takes to climb 1000 feet (300 m) over a distance of $\frac{1}{2}$ mile (800 m). For example, if Naismith's formula estimates a journey time of 9 hours and your fitness level is 25, you should allow 11.5 hours.

Additional adjustments for poor terrain or conditions can be estimated by dropping one or more fitness levels.

Individual fitness in minutes	Times taken in hours using Naismith's formula															
	2	**3**	**4**	**5**	**6**	**7**	**8**	**9**	**10**	**12**	**14**	**16**	**18**	**20**	**22**	**24**
15 very fit	1	1.5	2	2.25	3.5	4.5	5.5	6.75	7.75	10	12.5	14.5	17	19.5	22	24
20	1.25	2.25	3.25	4.5	5.5	6.5	7.75	8.75	10	12.5	15	17.5	20	23		
25	1.5	3	4.25	5.5	7	8.5	10	11.5	13.25	15	17.5					
30	2	3.5	5	6.75	8.5	10.5	12.5	14.5								
40	2.75	4.25	5.75	7.5	9.5	11.5			Too much to be attempted							
50 unfit	3.25	4.75	6.5	8.5												

Data Sheet Practice

You will need to use the data sheet for **By the left, quick march** to answer these questions.

1 A group of cadets go on an expedition.
The scale on their map is 1 cm : 50 000 cm.
If the cadets walk 1 cm on the map, what distance will they have really walked in kilometres?

2 The cadets walk 20 kilometres.
They climb 500 metres.
Use Naismith's formula to estimate how many minutes the expedition will take them.

3 For their second expedition they walk 18 kilometres.
They climb 1000 metres.
Use Naismith's formula to estimate how many minutes the second expedition will take them.

4 Ralph uses Naismith's formula to estimate that an expedition will take him 540 minutes.
He has a fitness level of 30.
Use Tranter's corrections to make a more accurate estimate of the time that the expedition will take him.

5 Sylvie has a fitness level of 20.
She walks 30 kilometres.
She climbs 600 metres.
How long will the walk take using Naismith's formula and Tranter's corrections?

6 The army cadets go on a different expedition.
They cover a distance of 25 kilometres.
It takes them 390 minutes.
Use Naismith's formula to estimate the height they climbed.

Data Sheet Questions

You will need to use the data sheet for **By the left, quick march** to answer these questions.

1 A group of army cadets go on three mountain expeditions.

a In expedition 1 they estimate that on the map their walk is 20 cm long.
The scale of their map is 1 cm : 50 000 cm.
What is the distance of their first expedition in kilometres?

(2 marks)

b For expedition 2 they estimate they will walk 16 km and climb 750 metres.
Using Naismith's formula, estimate how many minutes expedition 2 should take. *(2 marks)*

c On their final expedition the army cadets get lost while climbing the mountain.
They know that they have climbed 800 metres and that the walk took 260 minutes.
Use Naismith's formula to estimate the length of the walk.

(3 marks)

2 Three new army cadets are joining the group.
They complete some training walks.

a Callum has fitness level 25.
Using Naismith's formula he estimates that a walk will take 300 minutes.
Work out a more accurate estimate of how long Callum's walk should take. *(2 marks)*

b Alex has fitness level 30.
She is going on a level walk of 15 kilometres.
Estimate how long her walk will take. *(3 marks)*

c This table shows how Tranter's corrections can be adjusted.

20 kg load being carried	Drop one fitness level
Night	Drop one fitness level
Wind against	Drop one fitness level
Slippery/rocky terrain	Drop two fitness levels

Hasan has fitness level 15.
He is going on a 39 kilometre night walk.
During the walk he will climb 120 metres.
Hasan is planning to carry a 20 kg backpack.
Estimate how long Hasan will take to complete the walk. *(3 marks)*

Extension Questions

For the part of a journey that is downhill, Naismith's formula is more accurate if this correction is made:

Gentle downhill slope (angle less than 12°)	Subtract 10 minutes for every 300 metres of descent
Steep downhill slope (angle greater than 12°)	Add 10 minutes for every 300 metres of descent

On one expedition the cadets have a vertical descent of 900 metres over a horizontal distance of 4.5 kilometres.

1 Calculate the angle of descent.

2 Calculate the estimated time for the journey in hours and minutes.
Use the correction for the angle of descent.

3 Naismith's formula can be modified to take into account the angle of descent.
Rewrite Naismith's formula for a descent of h metres at an angle of greater than 12°.
Write this formula as simply as possible.

4 What is the distance that the cadets actually walk on this expedition?
Assume an even slope and that the cadets walk straight downhill.

E-traders

This table shows advertising fees for selling on the internet.

Advertising fees						
Insertion fees		**Pictures**			**Features**	
Price of item	**Fee**					
£0.01 – £0.99	£0.15	First picture	FREE		Subtitle	£ 0.45
£1.00 – £4.99	£0.20	Each additional picture	£0.12		Title in bold	£ 0.75
£5.00 – £14.99	£0.35				Highlight	£ 2.50
£15.00 – £29.99	£0.75				Special feature	£15.95
£30.00 – £99.99	£1.50					
£100.00 or more	£2.00					

1. Adam places an advert to sell a CD for £5.99.
   He pays for the title to be in bold and a subtitle.

   How much does Adam pay for the advert? *(2 marks)*

2. Matthew wants to advertise a computer for £225.
   He plans to spend between £12 and £15 on advertising fees.

   He is going to use a discount offer that gives him $\frac{1}{3}$ off the total fee.

   Give details of a possible advert that Matthew could use. *(3 marks)*

3. This table shows the numbers of registered users of an internet auction site. It also shows how many of these were active users on the internet site.

Numbers in millions			
	2003	2004	2005
Registered users	94.9	135.5	180.6
Active users	41.2	56.1	71.8

   a. Work out the number of registered users that were **not** active users in 2005. *(2 marks)*

   b. In 2003 the internet site started to send e-mails to registered users to try to persuade them to become active users.
   Is there any evidence to suggest that these e-mails were successful?
   You **must** show your working. *(3 marks)*

Extension Questions

1 Work out the percentage increase in **active** users from

a 2003 to 2004

b 2004 to 2005.

Give your answers to 3 significant figures.

2 Write the number of registered users in 2005 in standard form.

3 The number of registered users in 2003 was an increase of 45% on the number in 2002.
Work out the number of registered users in 2002.

4 The figures in the table for 2003 are given to 3 significant figures.
Find the maximum and minimum possible values of the number of registered users that were **not** active users.

5 Another website had 8.1×10^7 active users in 2005.
Find the difference in the number of active users on the two websites in 2005.
Give your answer in standard form.

Playing safe

Crèche groups

- A crèche may include more than one group of children.
  For children aged 2 years or over, the size of each group should not exceed 26 children.
  For children under 2 years, the size of each group should not exceed 12 children.

- At least half of all childcare staff should hold a level 2 qualification appropriate for the care or development of children.

- There should be one toilet and one wash hand basin for every 10 children over the age of 2 years.

Staffing ratios

Age	Minimum adult : child ratio
Children under 2 years	1 : 3
Children aged 2 years	1 : 4
Children aged 3–7 years	1 : 8

- There should always be a minimum of two adults on duty.

- Trainees under 17 years of age are supervised at all times and are not counted in staffing ratios; trainees of 17 years or over who are considered competent and responsible may be included in the staffing ratios.

- At least 50% of staff caring for babies/children under 2 years old should have received training in this specific area.

- Any care provided for children aged 8–14 should not adversely affect the care provided for children under 8 years old.

Space standards

Age	Minimum space per child
Children under 2 years	3.5 m^2
Children aged 2 years	2.5 m^2
Children aged 3–7 years	2.3 m^2

Data Sheet Practice

You will need to use the data sheet for **Playing safe** to answer these questions.

1 How many toilets should there be for a group of 26 children over the age of 2 years?

2 **a** What is the minimum adult : child ratio for a group of children who are all under 2 years old?

b What is the minimum number of adults for a group of 12 children who are all under 2 years old?

c How many of the adults in part (b) should have received training?

3 **a** What is the maximum number of children aged 2 years that can be looked after by three adults?

b (i) The diagram shows the dimensions of a room used for children aged 2 years. Calculate the area of this room.

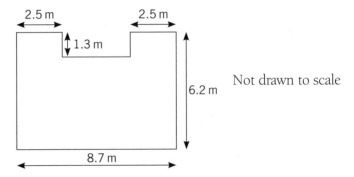

Not drawn to scale

(ii) What is the maximum number of children aged 2 years that can be looked after in this room?

c What is the maximum number of children aged 2 years that can be looked after in this room by four adults?

4 The table shows the expected costs of running the crèche.

Job	Number of staff	Hours worked	Salary
Manager	1	40 hours	£410 per week
Nursery nurses	5	40 hours each	£295 per week
Nursery assistants	7	24 hours each	£7.05 per hour

Other costs: £154 per week

a What is the total salary bill for one week?

b A market survey suggests that 72 children will use the crèche for an average of 15 hours per week.
How much does the crèche need to charge per child per hour to cover its costs?

Data Sheet Questions

You will need to use the data sheet for **Playing safe** to answer these questions.

1 **a** In a crèche there is a group of children who are all between 3 and 5 years old.
What is the minimum adult : child ratio for this group? *(1 mark)*

b In a crèche there is a group of 26 children who are all between 3 and 5 years old.
What is the minimum number of adults for this group? *(3 marks)*

2 In a different crèche, the staff on duty during one week is the manager, four nursery nurses and six assistants who each work 30 hours.

Job	Salary
Manager	£370 per week
Nursery nurses	£280 per week
Nursery assistants	£6.50 per hour

a What is the total salary bill for the week? *(3 marks)*

b During the week 75 children used the crèche for an average of 12 hours each.
The crèche charged a flat rate of £3.75 per child per hour.
How much did the crèche earn during the week? *(2 marks)*

c After paying salaries, how much does the crèche have left? *(1 mark)*

3 Mary plans to start a crèche using the room shown in the diagram below.

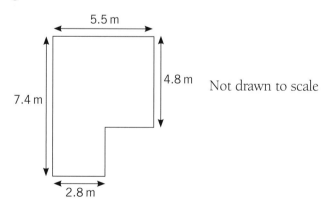

5.5 m
4.8 m   Not drawn to scale
7.4 m
2.8 m

She wants the crèche to open for 10 hours a day from Monday to Friday.
Give full details of **one** possible way that Mary might run the crèche.
Use the table of staffing costs in question 2. *(7 marks)*

Extension Questions

1 The crèche manager plans to use a new room of area 39 m² for a group of x children aged 2 years.

a (i) Write down an inequality in x.

(ii) Solve the inequality. What is the maximum number of children allowed in the room?

b Let y represent the number of adults looking after x children aged 2 years.

(i) Write down an inequality connecting x and y.

(ii) Use your answer for part (a)(ii) to find the minimum number of staff that are needed to look after this number of children.

2 The crèche is advertised in a local paper.

a This histogram shows the time the children spend in the crèche in a week **before** the advert appeared in the paper.

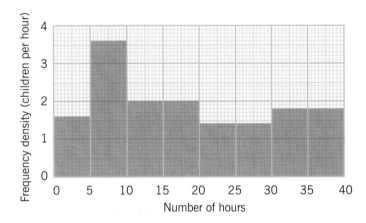

(i) Write down the modal group.

(ii) Work out the total number of children that are left at the crèche during this week.

(iii) Estimate the percentage of the children who spend more than 24 hours in the crèche.

b The table shows the time the children spend in the crèche in a week **after** the advert appeared in the paper.

(i) What is the modal group?

(ii) Calculate an estimate of the mean time spent per child in the crèche.

(iii) Explain why your answer to part (b)(ii) is an estimate, rather than an accurate value.

(iv) Draw a histogram to illustrate the data given in the table.

Number of hours in crèche (x)	Frequency (f)
$0 < x \leq 5$	25
$5 < x \leq 10$	19
$10 < x \leq 20$	21
$20 < x \leq 30$	14
$30 < x \leq 40$	18
Total	**97**

c Compare the histograms from parts (a) and (b).
Did the advert in the local paper have an effect on the number of children using the crèche? Explain your answer.

Student loans

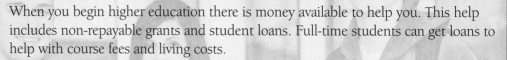

When you begin higher education there is money available to help you. This help includes non-repayable grants and student loans. Full-time students can get loans to help with course fees and living costs.

Course fees

Fees cost a maximum of £3145 per year for courses that begin in September 2008. However, course fees are likely to increase each year with inflation. Full loans are available for course fees.

Living costs

Loans are available to help with your living costs. The amount of loan that you are allowed to take out depends on:

● where you live while you study
● your total household income.

The amounts you can borrow are shown in this table.

Where you live to do the course		Maximum loan for ...	
		A full year	The final year
Away from home	In London	£6475	£5895
Away from home	Outside London	£4625	£4280
At home		£3580	£3235

1. Tom plans to do an Honours degree in History at the University of Durham starting in September 2008.
   Here is some information about Tom's course fees and living costs.
   ● Course fees for September 2008 are £3145.
   ● Tom is eligible for the maximum loan for living costs.
   ● Tom plans to live away from home.
   What is the maximum amount that Tom can borrow to finance the first year of his course? *(2 marks)*

2. Tina plans to do a two-year Foundation degree in Fashion. She wants to do this at New College Nottingham starting in September 2008.
   Here is some information about course fees and living costs.
   ● Course fees for September 2008 are £2095.
   ● Course fees for September 2009 are likely to increase by 3% with inflation.
   ● Tina's household income means that she is eligible for only 75% of the maximum loan for living costs.
   ● The loan for living costs does not increase with inflation.
   ● Tina plans to live at home.
   Tina plans to borrow as much as she can.
   Work out an estimate of the total amount she plans to borrow to finance the whole course. *(5 marks)*

3 You start repaying your loan in the April following the completion of your course.

The rate of repayment is 9% of any income you earn more than £15 000 per year.

- Tom starts work in the September after he completes his course in June.
- His salary is £23 520 per year.
- He is paid monthly.

How much of his student loan does he repay in the first year that he works?

(3 marks)

Extension Questions

1 You are charged interest on your student loan from the day you receive it.
The interest rate is the same as the rate of inflation.

a What does this tell you about the real value of what you owe?
Here is how you can estimate how much you will owe at the end of your course.
1. *Assume an inflation rate of, say, 3%*
2. *Assume that course fees increase each year in line with inflation.*
3. *Assume that the loan for any year is paid in full at the start of that year.*
4. *Add 3% compound interest to your loan for each year you receive it.*

b Look at the information about Tom from question 1 on page 76.
Tom completes the course, which takes three years.
How much does Tom owe at the end of his course?

c Why is the estimate in 1(b) an overestimate?

2 The calculation you did in 1(b) will only give a rough idea of interest charges.
The reason for this is that interest is actually charged **daily**.
The daily interest rate used is equivalent to the yearly inflation rate.
Assume that the inflation rate is 3% per year.
Work out the equivalent daily interest rate.

Positive and negative numbers

(1) Work out the length of this stick.

```
       ░░░░░░░░░░░░░░░░░░░░░░░░░░░░░░░░░
 |||||||||||||||||||||||||||||||||||||||||||||||||||||||
 0    1    2    3    4    5    6    7    8    9   10   11
  cm
```

(2) The balance in Jan's bank account is –£32.
What is the balance after her wage of £154 is added?

(3) The temperature at midday was 3°C. The temperature at midnight was –8°C.
Work out the difference between the temperature at midnight and midday?

(4) Marshville is 25 metres below sea level.
The lookout tower in Marshville is
34 metres high.

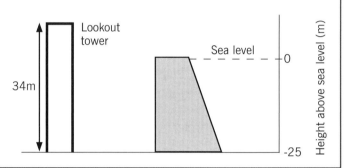

How high above sea level is the top
of the lookout tower?

Calculations with numbers of any size

(1) Packets of biscuits cost 89p each.
Alfie buys four packets of biscuits.
How much change does he get from a £5 note?

(2) A Physics lesson starts at 2:20 pm.
It lasts for three quarters of an hour.
What time does the lesson finish?

(3) 1 euro (€)= £0.65
Convert €25 to pounds.

(4) A charity starts a fund-raising campaign.
Their target is to raise $\frac{1}{4}$ million pounds.
After one week they have raised £20 225.
How much more do they need to meet their target?

(5) DVDs are 15 mm wide.
Work out the largest number of DVDs
that can fit on this shelf.

Ratio and proportion

① £50 is to be shared in the ratio 2 : 3
How much is the biggest share?

② Cakes are made using flour, fat and sugar in a ratio 2 : 1 : 1
100 g of flour is used.
How much fat is used?

③ Sam mixes red and white paint in the ratio 1 : 4 to make pink paint.
He wants to make 20 litres of pink paint.
How much red paint should he use?

④ The menu shows the ingredients for making a pizza base for two people.

> **Pizza base (2 people)**
> 100 g flour
> 60 ml water
> 4 g yeast
> 20 ml milk
> salt

How many grams of yeast do I need for a pizza base for five people?

Fractions, decimals and percentages

① Tom scores 36 out of 200 marks in a test. Work out his score as a percentage.

② Ann saves 15% of what she earns.
What fraction of what she earns does Ann save?

③ Write the fractions $\frac{2}{3}$, $\frac{3}{5}$, $\frac{11}{15}$ and $\frac{21}{30}$ in order from lowest to highest.

④ Put these in order of size starting with the smallest.
0.5   20% $\frac{1}{6}$ $\frac{1}{4}$ 0.3

⑤ Here is a box of chocolates.
One chocolate has been eaten.
What fraction of the chocolates has been eaten?

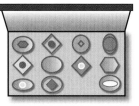

⑥ There are 60 sweets in a bag of sweets. Tom eats 30% of the sweets.
Emma eats $\frac{1}{3}$ of the sweets.
Work out the number of sweets left in the bag.

Add and subtract fractions

1 Jack eats one quarter of a cake. Jill eats one third of the same cake.
What fraction of the whole cake do Jack and Jill eat?

2 Annie eats $\frac{1}{4}$ of a pizza. Brian eats $\frac{1}{5}$ of the same pizza.
How much of the pizza is left?

3 Thieves steal $\frac{1}{2}$ of the money from a bank.
They drop $\frac{1}{3}$ of the money that they steal.
What fraction of the bank money do the thieves still have?

4 This table shows the fraction of a class that live in different sorts of accommodation.

Type of home	Detached house	Semi-detached house	Terraced house	Flat	Boat
Fraction of class	$\frac{1}{15}$	$\frac{1}{6}$	$\frac{8}{15}$	$\frac{1}{5}$	$\frac{1}{30}$

What is the total fraction of the class that live in houses?

Add, subtract, multiply and divide decimals

1 Petrol costs 94.9 pence per litre.
Dipak puts 20 litres of petrol in his car.
Work out the cost of this petrol.

2 A 5 kilogram cheese is cut into equal weight pieces.
Each piece of cheese weighs 0.2 kg.
Work out the total number of pieces.

3 A burger costs £1.24
A portion of chips cost 79p.
Sauce costs 5p.
Work out the total cost of a burger, a portion of chips and sauce.

4 A sprinter runs 100 metres in 9.866 seconds.
Round this to 2 decimal places.

5 The total land area of the Netherlands is 33 812 km².
Round this area to the nearest 1000 km².

Equations and formulae

1 You are given that c represents the cost of a cup of coffee in pence.
Two cups of coffee cost 50 pence.
Write down an equation in terms of c.

2 What is the missing value in the table?

800 watts	600 watts
1 min	1 min 20 sec
2 min	2 min 40 sec
3 min	
6 min	8 min
9 min	12 min

3 Solve the equation $2x - 7 = 3$

4 Here are some shapes made using white and grey tiles.

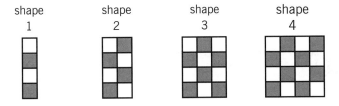

shape 1   shape 2   shape 3   shape 4

How many white tiles will there be in shape number 10?

5 $4y = 20$. Write down the value of y^2.

6 The cost, £C, of hiring a boat for h hours is worked out using the formula
$C = 5 + 3h$.
Work out how much it costs to hire the boat for 2 hours.

7 A factory uses the formula $W = 25 + 10h$ to work out the waste, W kg, for a time of t hours.
Work out the waste for a time of 6 hours.

8 A taxi firm uses the formula $F = 2.4 + 2m$ to work out the fare, £F, for a journey of m miles.
Work out the fare for a journey of 3.4 miles.

2-D representations of 3-D objects

1 Opposite faces on a dice add up to 7.
This is the net of a dice.

What is the number on the face labelled A?

2 Which **two** diagrams are the nets of a triangular based prism?

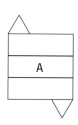 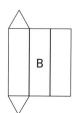 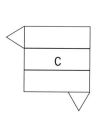 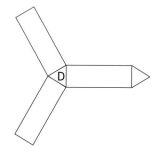

3 This solid is made from six centimetre cubes.

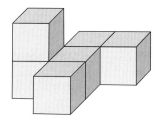

Which one of the following shows the side elevation of the solid?

    A   B   C   D

4 The diagram shows the side view of a solid shape.
Which of these shapes could it be?
(a) cone
(b) cylinder
(c) cube
(d) cuboid

Area, perimeter and volume

1 The length of the side of a regular pentagon is 11 cm.
Work out its perimeter.

2 Work out the area of this triangle.

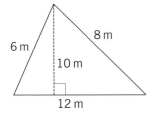

3 The length of the side of a cube is 3 centimetres.
Calculate the volume of the cube.

4 A tin of paint covers 12 m². The area of a wall is 38 m².
How many tins of paint are needed to paint the wall?

5 Work out the volume of this prism.

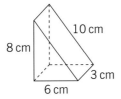

6 This container is in the form of a trapezium-based prism.
Use the formula $V = AL$ to work out the volume of the container.

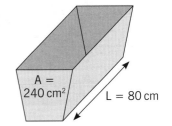

7 A rectangle has an area of 24 cm² and a perimeter of 22 cm.
Write down the length and width of the rectangle.

8 Cylindrical tins of radius 4 cm and height 5 cm are placed in the box
with dimensions as shown.

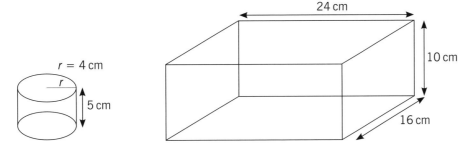

What is the maximum number of tins that can be placed in the box?

Dimensions using scale

1 A map has a scale of 1 : 1000
On the map, a field has length 4 centimetres.
Work out the actual length of the field.
Give your answer in metres.

2 The scale on a map is 4 centimetres to 1 kilometre.
The distance between two villages on the map is 12 centimetres.
Work out the actual distance between the villages.
Give your answer in kilometres.

3 The diagram shows a scale drawing of a corridor.
The corridor is 2.5 metres wide.

2.5 m

Work out the length of the corridor in metres.

4 A model of a jumbo jet has a wingspan of 6 centimetres.
The jumbo jet has a wingspan of 60 metres.
Which one of the following represents the scale?

A 1 : 6000   B 1 : 1000   C 1 : 60 000   D 1 : 10 000

Metric and imperial units

1 A plane travels at a speed of 600 miles per hour.
Work out how far it travels in 20 minutes.

2 A car travels at a speed of 16 miles in 15 minutes.
Work out the speed in miles per hour.

3 The diagram shows a gauge for a petrol tank.
The tank holds 8 gallons when full.
Work out the number of gallons of petrol
left in the tank.

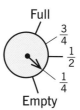

4 **5 miles = 8 kilometres**
Susan cycles for 15 miles.
Jenny cycles for 25 km.
Who cycles further?

Collect and record discrete and continuous data

1. The tally chart shows the number of milkshakes a shop sells in one weekend.

	Number of milkshakes
Chocolate	ⵦⵦ ⵦⵦ ⵦⵦ ||
Strawberry	ⵦⵦ ⵦⵦ ||
Vanilla	ⵦⵦ ⵦⵦ
Lemon	||
Orange	ⵦⵦ ||||

How many strawberry milkshakes does the shop sell?

2. Tim collects this data about how 10 students travel to school.

David	Walk
Mary	Bus
Emma	Walk
Barry	Car
Duncan	Bus
Sally	Walk
Susan	Car
Tony	Walk
Peter	Bus
Steven	Walk

Copy and complete the two-way table to show this data.

	Walk	Bus	Car
Boy	3		1
Girl		1	1

Frequency diagrams, pie charts and scatter diagrams

1 The pie chart shows the composition of different materials which are collected in a district's household recycling boxes.

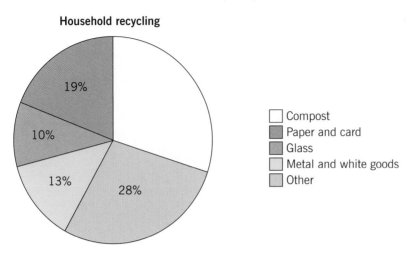

What percentage of household recycling is made up of compost?

2 The graph shows the times of sunrise and sunset for different dates.

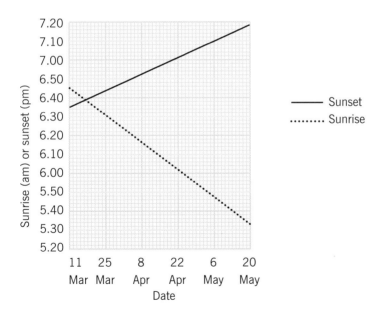

What time was sunset on the 22 April?

Statistical methods

1. Five numbers have a mean of 20.
   What is the total of the five numbers?

2. The stem-and-leaf diagram shows the time spent on homework in a term
   by 11 students in a school.

   Key: $1 \mid 9$ represents 19 hours

   ```
   1 | 8 9 9
   2 | 3 5 7 8 9
   3 | 3 7 8
   4 |
   ```

   What is the median time that these students spent on homework?

Probability scale from 0 to 1

1. Assad bought 5 raffle tickets.
   There were 500 raffle tickets sold altogether.
   What is the probability that Assad wins?

2. The probability that it rains today is 0.3
   What is the probability that it does not rain?

3. This two-way table shows how 9 boys and 11 girls travel to school.

	Walk	Bus	Car
Boy	2	4	3
Girl	6	3	2

   One of the boys is picked at random.
   What is the probability that he walks to school?